THE DARWEN COUNTY HISTORY SERIES

A History of
BERKSHIRE

As in many Victorian towns, behind the fine buildings on the main streets was a maze of alleys and mean streets.

THE DARWEN COUNTY HISTORY SERIES

A History of
BERKSHIRE

Judith Hunter

Phillimore

1995

Published by
PHILLIMORE & CO. LTD.
Shopwyke Manor Barn, Chichester, West Sussex

ISBN 0 85033 729 1

Printed and bound in Great Britain by
BUTLER & TANNER LTD.
London and Frome

Contents

Acknowledgements

Since 1974, when the county boundaries were changed to include Slough, Berkshire has been my adopted county. But after researching and writing on various aspects of the history of the Slough and Windsor area for several years, I found that the research for this book on the county proved a very different kind of challenge. It was not so much a matter of research using original records, but one of reading and assimilating 'all' that had been written. To all those authors whose books and articles I read I to dedicate this book.

I should also like to express my appreciation of the many historians and archaeologists who so willingly gave of their time and help and made the work for this book a pleasure: Dennis Ayres, Roy Brigden, Eugene Burden, Andrew French, Peter Frensham, Tony Higgott, Kerr Kirkwood, Pamela Knight, Don Miller, Ted Sammes, and Angela Tuddenham. My thanks also go to Michael Bayley, Helen Cooper, Daphne Fido, Janet Gammon, Colin Woodward, the Twyford and Ruscombe Local History Society, and the Windsor Local History Publication Group whose line drawings enliven the pages, and to Jack Neave who turned my sketches into maps. I give thanks also to the many other individuals, and the staff of the libraries, museums and record offices listed below, who helped me to choose photographs, and finally, but certainly not least, I should like to thank my husband and Professor Alan Rogers for their help and encouragement.

The following have given their permission to reproduce illustrations: The Royal Collection © Her Majesty the Queen, 32; Berkshire County Council, 14; Berkshire Record Office, 112; Oxfordshire Photographic Archive, DLA, 7, 39, 105; Chippenham Library, 80; the Master and Fellows, Magdalene College, Cambridge, 65; Museum of Reading, 140; Public Record Office, 81; Royal Borough Collection, 52, 60, 61, 64, 73, 75, 77, 110, 117, 120, 143; Royal County of Berkshire: Cultural Services: Library and Information Service, 2, 9, 28, 58, 66, 67, 74, 87, 88, 96-8, 106, 107, 109, 111, 115, 116; Rural History Centre, University of Reading, 10, 34, 57, 72, 94, 95, 99, 108, 114, 119, 121, 122, 130, 133, 136, 137, 138; Slough Museum, 128, 131; Trust for Wessex Archaeology, 13, 17, 41; Vale and Downland Museum, frontispiece, 104, 123; Peter Ballinger, 70; Anne Darrencourt, 54; R.G. Martin, 86; Hugh Pihlens, 63, 85; Michael Bayley, 19, 20, 23, 25, 26, 27, 49, 53, 55, 56, 76, 93, 132, 134, 135; Helen Cooper, 40, 51, 59; Daphne Fido, 5, 45, 71, 78; Janet Gammon, 113; Jack Neave, 1, 3, 4, 18, 21, 29, 33, 36, 42, 43, 44, 48, 84, 103, 129; David Poynter, 89, 90; Colin Woodward, 35; Twyford and Ruscombe Local History Society, 24, 82, 83, 125, 139, 141, 142; Windsor Local History Publication Group, 30, 31.

Beautiful Berkshire, I, IX, XI; Ivan Belcher Colour Picture Library, II, V, VI, VIII, X, XII, XIV, XV.

List of Illustrations

List of Colour Illustrations

Introduction

Berkshire Old and New—In Search of the County

Colnbrook became part of Berkshire on 1 April 1995; it was the most recent of the many county boundary changes that have taken place over the past thousand years—and the last change before the county disappears as an administrative unit. The heart of the original shire, created in the mid-Saxon period, lay in the Vale of the White Horse. But the Berkshire of those times did not include the eastern part of the present county; this area did not become part of the county until the tenth century. The county which was then formed survived, except for minor boundary adjustments, until 1974. For the inhabitants of the parishes concerned, however, these small changes could bring very important changes indeed—be they differences in taxes, local government policies, the way in which justice was administered, or merely a change in loyalties.

The very irregular shape of the ancient boundary in the extreme south west, together with its relationship to field patterns, suggests that here the county boundary was drawn long after the local communities had determined their territory, and was a matter of local determination. In the 11th century, parts of the parishes of Shalbourne and Hungerford lay in Wiltshire, but sometime later in the Middle Ages Shalbourne became part of Berkshire and is shown on the early county maps as a curious meandering extension to the main body of the county. In 1894 it was transferred to

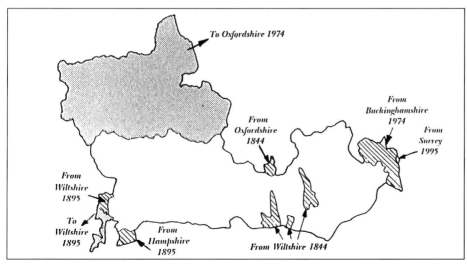

1 *Berkshire Old and New. The map depicts the county as it never existed in order to show the main areas lost or added to the county in the last 200 years.*

2 *Wiltshire Road in Wokingham is a reminder that Berkshire once included several areas within its boundaries that were part of the county of Wiltshire whose residents answered to the authorities of that county.*

Wiltshire. Under the same Act of Parliament Combe parish was transferred from Hampshire to Berkshire, together with parts of Hungerford which for centuries had belonged to Wiltshire. At last this corner of the county took on its present shape.

The Norman lordship of Faringdon included outliers, detached parts of the estate, at Little Faringdon and Shilton within Oxfordshire and at Barrington in Gloucestershire. At some time in the Middle Ages parts of the parishes of Barkham, Hurst, Swallowfield and Sonning became outliers of Wiltshire lying within Berkshire, a result of grants to the Manor of Amesbury of land in Windsor Forest. Such detached portions of county areas were abolished in 1844. In 1894 part of New Hinksey in Oxfordshire came into Berkshire and in 1911 the Oxfordshire village of Caversham, which had by then become a fashionable suburb of Reading, was also transferred to Berkshire.

There have been other minor changes, but these were eclipsed by those wrought under the 1974 Local Government Act. As a result of this, a very large area in the north west, arguably the most ancient part of the county, was given to Oxfordshire, in 'exchange' for the southern tip of Buckinghamshire. Three years later Caversham and Slough were once again enlarged at the expense of their old counties. Twenty years on there are still those who regret the recent changes. But roots have grown and new allegiances formed, and many will mourn if Berkshire is lost as an administrative county through the government's restructuring policies. But as long as people care about the past, the county name will live on; this book concerns the story of all those Berkshires, old and new.

1

Man and the Natural Landscape

The story of Berkshire can be said to have begun some 130 million years ago in the Jurassic period with the formation of its oldest rocks beneath the waves of an ancient sea. The earliest of these Jurassic rocks is the Oxford Clay, a bed of dark grey clay, some 450 feet thick, which underlies the Upper Thames Valley. To the south successively younger strata run in more or less parallel bands east-west across the county with the youngest rocks in the extreme south-east corner. These are the Bagshot Beds, mainly infertile sands and clays which were laid down in another sea, some 60 million years ago in the Eocene era.

Many forces have played a rôle in shaping the Berkshire landscape, but not least were the earth movements which built the Alps and whose 'outer ripples' gently folded the rocks of southern Britain to form the London Basin and the anticlines of the Weald, Hampshire and the Chilterns. It was

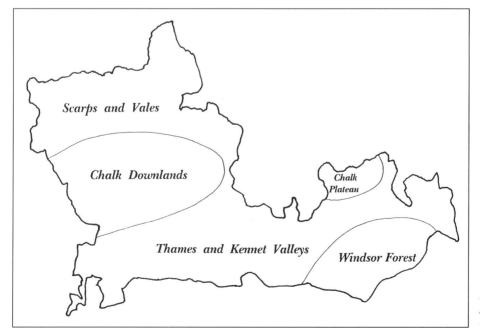

3 *The major topographical regions of Berkshire.*

13

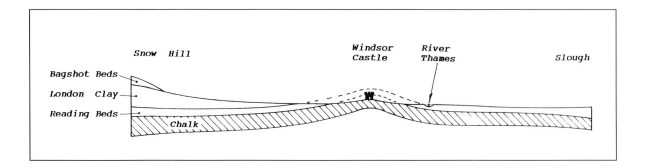

Snow Hill   *Windsor Castle*   *River Thames*   *Slough*

Bagshot Beds
London Clay
Reading Beds
Chalk

4 *Geological section across eastern Berkshire showing the chalk upfold on which Windsor Castle stands.*

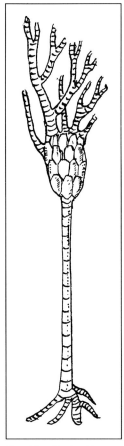

5 *A fossil crinoid or sea lily found in limestone.*

these earth movements which gave Berkshire its basic topography, for much of the county lies on the western edge of the London Basin, and almost all its geological strata dip south and south-eastward. The folding, however, created many minor crests and valleys, and here and there small upfolds have brought older rocks to the surface. The most notable example of this is the isolated chalk hill on which Windsor Castle stands. In north-west Berkshire, the tilting of successive bands of soft clays and harder limestones and sandstone has given rise to a landscape of vales, steep scarps and gentle dip slopes. Immediately south of the Upper Thames Valley is a low line of hills known to geologists as the Corallian Ridge from the fossil corals found in its limestone beds. Its scarp faces the Thames, but on the south the hills have a more gentle slope, gradually merging into the Vale of the White Horse. Two bands of clay, the Kimmeridge and Gault Clays, form the Vale which stretches across almost the whole of this part of the old county, from Shrivenham to Abingdon. The Vale is drained by the slow-flowing River Ock, and its flat, clay valley bottom is more than five miles wide in places. In dramatic contrast is its southern boundary where Upper Greensand and chalk form a series of terraces and steep scarps, above which lie the Berkshire Downs and the ancient chalk figure which has given the Vale its name.

Chalk covers more than a quarter of the county, from the high downland in the north and west to the gentle hills of the country between Wargrave and Maidenhead. Scenically perhaps, the Berkshire Downs are the most impressive part of the old county. Although nowhere do the crests rise much above 800 feet, the level hill tops are deeply dissected by numerous steep-sided dry valleys. The flat areas between are the remnants of ancient uplifted land surfaces, and the valleys are the relics of a vast drainage system that was most effective at the end of the Ice Ages. The present Lambourn River is a 'mere trunk' of a much larger river system that has been shrinking for the last 10,000 years. The upper levels of the chalk are waterless, and the wide expanses of springy turf seem to be one of its most characteristic features. Yet weathering has produced an extensive deposit known as clay-with-flints which is more fertile than chalk soils and once supported woodland.

Separated from the main chalk hills by the River Kennet is another area of chalk where Berkshire takes in a small part of the North Hampshire Downs. Rising steeply from the valley, the downs here reach their greatest

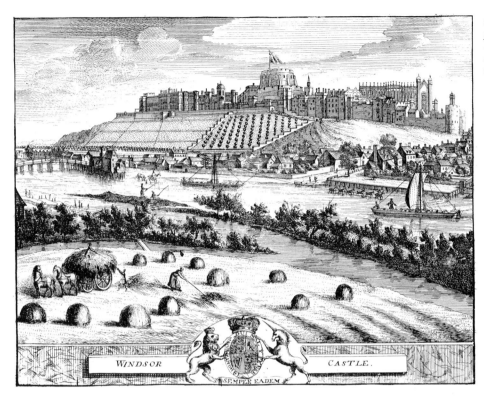

heights at Inkpen Beacon and Walbury Camp. The latter at 975 feet is the highest point on chalk anywhere in Britain; the views across the Kennet valley are superb.

The eastern area of chalk is very different. The surface is a much lower plateau with the great bend of the Thames forming an incised meander on three sides. Its steep edge can be most easily appreciated at Remenham and Winter Hill at Cookham. The chalk here has no dry valleys, and its topography is unremarkable except for two conical hills—Bowsey Hill and Ashley Hill—both capped by Upper Greensand. Although only some 450 feet high, they can be seen from long distances.

In the south of the county the oldest of the geological formations belonging to the Eocene period are known as the Reading Beds, a mixed clay and sandy strata which forms a discontinuous band of gentle hilly country across the county from Hungerford to Bray. More distinctive, perhaps, is the London Clay which covers a large area of eastern Berkshire, from Arborfield to Windsor, and a rather smaller area around Burghfield and Mortimer with narrow extensions further west. It forms a moderately fertile, but heavy soil, and is practically impervious to water. In contrast are the formations collectively known as the Bagshot Beds which give rise to sandy, well drained, but infertile soils. They underlie an area known until the 19th century as Bagshot Heath which, according to William Cobbett, was 'as bleak, as barren, and as villainous a heath as ever man set his eyes on'.

7 View of a wide expanse of the flat tops of the Berkshire Downs, c.1900.

The Kennet and Thames Valleys are as distinctive a feature of Berkshire's topography as the scarp of the Downs, although the spread of roads and houses has diminished their physical impact on our senses. Both rivers meander over a flood plain covered by recent deposits of alluvium and river gravels. Here the difference of only a few feet was important to earlier settlers for it was the difference between marshy land which was frequently flooded and land which usually stood above the flood water. Reading was founded on a large gravel terrace cut through by the Kennet, and the sites of several of the villages in the valleys were at least partly determined by the gravel deposits. In the east of the county the gravels extend up the dip slope of the Chilterns in a series of terraces formed during the Ice Ages. They are most easily recognised between Maidenhead and Colnbrook, where much of the original research into Thames terraces has been carried out.

Each terrace marks a warm period during the Ice Ages, and each drop to the next terrace is the result of down-cutting by the Thames during the cold periods when sea levels were much lower. Thick layers of gravel accumulated on the flood plain during the warm interglacials, and during the last of the glacial periods when southern Britain was subject to tundra conditions wind-blown material, known as brickearth, was deposited on the lower terraces. None of the ice sheets reached as far south as Berkshire, but originally the Thames had flowed in a more northerly route through the Chilterns, and twice its valley was blocked by a glacier. The river was forced

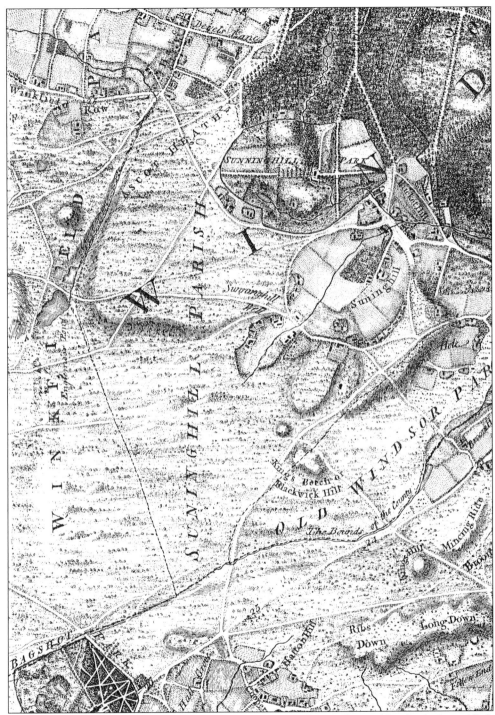

8 *Jean Rocque's map of Berkshire of 1761 showing part of the 'villainous' heath which straddled the Berkshire/Surrey border.*

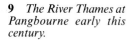

9 *The River Thames at Pangbourne early this century.*

to change course and flow further south, leaving behind the series of ter-races. Similar river terraces are also found all along the Thames Valley, and in the Kennet and Loddon Valleys.

The First Inhabitants

The Ice Ages lasted some two million years during which time the ice sheets advanced and retreated several times. Sometime during this era man came to live in Britain and to make his home in Berkshire. The oldest human remains belong to a period known as the Hoxnian Interglacial (425,000 to 360,000 BC) when birch, pine and oak woods covered much of the land and gave shelter to such animals as red deer, hippopotamus, bison, aurochs and cave lions. Remains of them have been found in the Thames river gravels at Swanscombe in Kent, but much older flint tools found elsewhere in the country are evidence that Britain had already been inhabited for more than 100,000 years before the Hoxnian period. Early man may also have lived through the cold conditions of a glacial period when such creatures as woolly rhinoceroses and mammoths roamed the grassland steppes.

No human remains from such remote periods have been found in Berkshire, but the Thames Valley gravels have been a rich source of flint implements and there is no doubt that bands of hunters inhabited the area during a period known in archaeological terms as the Lower Palaeolithic, or Lower Old Stone Age. The climate was temperate and riverside sites provided the inhabitants with a diversity of habitats—open water, swamp, grassland and woodland—and a rich variety of game. The Thames at this

10 *The Vale of the White Horse against the backdrop of the chalk scarp, the White Horse figure and the hill fort known as Uffington Castle.*

time had many channels and meandered through a wide flood plain, and small groups of people most likely occupied camp sites near the river. There were no caves to provide a convenient home, but Palaeolithic Man had the skills to build simple shelters. The sheer quantity of finds from the river gravel terraces between Maidenhead and Slough attests to the occupation of the area for many generations. Smaller numbers of palaeolithic tools have been found in many other parts of Berkshire, but there is a notable absence of finds from the chalk downlands.

The different types and styles of the flint tools give us some clues about the people living in Berkshire at this remote period. The oldest types of tools are those known as Clactonian after the place where they were first identified, and numerous examples of their core choppers and flake tools have been found at Caversham and in the gravels of the Boyne Hill terrace around Maidenhead. More prolific in Berkshire are the flint implements known as Acheulian. They were made by a people with a different culture who specialised in the manufacture of hand axes. Many of them were beautifully worked and they are a lasting proof of the skill and knowledge of the men who made them. The largest hand axe ever found in England was discovered unimpaired in a pit near Cannon Court Farm at Maidenhead. It is so large it cannot have been a working tool, but perhaps it had some special ritual significance. Hand axes were used to butcher animals, but

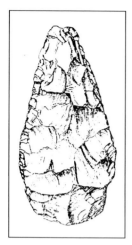

11   *The largest known Acheulian hand-axe was found at Furze Platt, Maidenhead in 1919. It is over 12 inces long.*

Palaeolithic Man had a range of tools. Flakes and cleavers were used to cut the flesh, and scrapers to clean the skin before it could be used for clothes and other purposes. Other implements were used as missiles, for grinding, and as wedges for splitting stones, bones and wood.

Over the thousands of years of the Palaeolithic period, man himself evolved and developed new skills, became more specialised, and adapted to different conditions. While the Acheulians appear to have retreated from Britain during the cold periods, men who produced Levalloisian flake tools lived in the tundra zone beyond the edge of the ice sheet. Eventually, however, during the last glacial period arctic conditions prevailed and Britain became uninhabitable.

This last glaciation (known as the Devensian) lasted an immensely long time and there were several relatively warmer periods within it during which people returned to Britain. Conditions were far from congenial and the total population of Great Britain at any one time may have been no more than a few hundred. At last, about 14,000 years ago the ice began to retreat for the last time and the sub-arctic conditions gave way to tundra and cold steppe grasslands—a treeless landscape. Once again Palaeolithic Man returned to this country, bringing with him a culture which has been named by archaeologists as Creswellian. These were Upper Palaeolithic people, and the majority of their known occupation sites in Britain are in caves, but there were a few open sites, including ones at Thatcham and Avington, near Hungerford. Man was still a hunter, and it may not be too fanciful to suppose that his pursuit of migratory herds of reindeer and horses determined the best crossing points of rivers and made tracks which were the beginning of our roads.

With the end of the Ice Ages and the return of a more hospitable climate in about 10,000 BC, the land took on a new green appearance as trees, grasses and herbaceous plants moved in from more southerly latitudes. England was still joined to the Continent and thus there was no barrier to the relatively rapid colonisation of the land by forest animals and plants. Birchwood replaced the grasslands, followed by pine woods and then deciduous trees such as hazel, elm, oak, alder and lime. By about 5,500 BC, the greater part of Berkshire, like most of the rest of lowland Britain, was covered by a mixed oak forest, inhabited by deer, elk, wild boars and aurochs and a great range of other woodland creatures. Gone were the great herds of easily culled reindeer and other migratory animals which had been so important to men of the late Old Stone Age. The people who now made Berkshire their home had to exploit a very different habitat, hunting individual animals rather than herds. These people of the Mesolithic, or Middle Stone Age, were hunters, fishermen and gatherers. Their tools were more diverse, and greater use was made of small flint blades known as microliths. Great quantities of their tools have been found at Thatcham where Mesolithic people used the same area for nearly a thousand years. They were mainly marsh or lake-side dwellers, and it is likely that they made their way inland following the rivers until they found sites to their liking. Bones show that the Thatcham people enjoyed a

Time Chart I

I Prehistoric Man

Archaeological Ages	Approximate date for the beginning of each Age	Approximate duration of each Age
Iron Age	600 BC	640 years
Bronze Age	2,300 BC	1,700 years
Neolithic Age	4,000 BC	1,700 years
Mesolithic Age	10,000 BC	6,000 years
Palaeolithic Age	400,000 BC	390,000 years

II Prehistoric Man and the Ice Ages

Divisions of the Ice Ages	Climate	Possible date for the beginning of each division	Duration of each division	Archaeological periods
Flandrian	WARM	14,000 years ago	14,000 years	MESOLITHIC to the present day #
Devensian (a major glaciation)	COLD with warm periods	115,000	110,000	UPPER * PALAEOLITHIC
Ipswichian	WARM	130,000	15,000	MIDDLE ** PALAEOLITHIC
Wolstonian	COLD with warm periods	360,000	130,000	
Hoxnian	WARM	425,000	65,000	
Anglian (a major glaciation)	COLD	480,000	55,000	LOWER PALAEOLITHIC
Cromerian	COOL	525,000	45,000	

*	Britain was unoccupied during part of the Devensian glaciation
**	It is not certain that Britain was occupied during the Ipswichian period
#	As the climate became warmer the levels of the seas rose and about 7,500 years ago Britain was separated from the Continent with the formation of the English Channel

varied diet which included deer, boar, fish, birds, wild ox and even horse, and hunted such animals as beaver, fox, badger and wild cats for their fur. Bones of dogs suggest that perhaps the dog was already partly domesticated and assisted man in hunting. The flint for their tools came from the river gravels and the chalk downs some five miles to the north west.

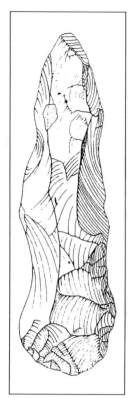

12 *A Mesolithic Thames pick from Maidenhead.*

13 *An imaginary scene: Mesolithic Man in the Kennet Valley.*

Although a very important site because of the richness of the archaeological finds, Thatcham is not the only Mesolithic site in Berkshire. About fifty have been found in the Kennet Valley between Thatcham and Hungerford, others at Holyport and the Abingdon area of the Upper Thames Valley, and along the Colne Valley just beyond the Berkshire boundary. Mesolithic hunters also lived on the chalk slopes overlooking the River Kennet.

How many communities lived in Berkshire during this period we call the Middle Stone Age is impossible to know, but what evidence there is suggests that each community was small, probably no larger than one or two families, and that the sites were occupied for only part of the year. Yet, in spite of their small numbers and nomadic way of life, it was Mesolithic Man who began the long process of transforming the landscape. Using fire and tools known today as Thames Picks, they began to enlarge the forest glades by the slash and burn method. The process of forest clearance had begun, especially where the tree cover was lightest on the river gravels.

The First Farmers

About 6,000 years ago a new type of people began moving into Britain from northern France. They came as small scattered groups over a long period, and there is no reason to suppose that they came as invaders or that they immediately replaced the older culture. They were, however, technologically more advanced and inevitably their way of life brought great changes. These Neolithic, or New Stone Age, people were farmers, and they brought with them seeds and the knowledge of plant cultivation, the skills to domesticate animals and to make pottery. Like the people already living in Britain, they hunted and gathered food, but their way of life was a more settled one, and the remains of their farmhouses, fields and burial sites have been found in many parts of Berkshire.

Although their polished stone axes made the work of felling small trees easier than the tools of earlier periods, they also favoured the light well-drained soils which were easiest to clear of trees, such as the river gravels in the Thames, Kennet, Loddon, Blackwater and Ock Valleys. Where they settled in sufficient numbers, they brought about a permanent clearance of the woodland. This came about, not because there were large numbers of settlers clearing huge areas, but because their method of farming involved clearing an area of ground and cultivating it until the soil was exhausted. They then moved to a new site and cleared this while their animals grazing on the abandoned fields prevented a return to woodland conditions.

Scattered finds of tools and pottery sherds suggest that there were few parts of the county shunned by Neolithic Man, but most of the occupation sites have been found in the valleys. Those at Abingdon, Remenham and Cannon Hill, Maidenhead have been identified as early Neolithic. At Runnymede Bridge, just across the county boundary, numerous pits, post holes and water-logged timbers are evidence of a fairly substantial village which flourished in the Middle Neolithic period. In contrast the remains of the settlement found at Burghfield would appear to be much later. Here the finds include the remains of a hearth, and it is thought that the single homestead was built in a small grassy clearing in oak and hazel woodland.

Neolithic Man left other evidence of his presence in Berkshire in the form of ditches, banks and earthworks which fulfilled a variety of functions. Parallel lines of ditches known as a cursus are thought to have had some ceremonial function. One discovered in Dorset is over six miles long, but, although there are none of this length in Berkshire, the cursus near Drayton in north Berkshire was the first ever discovered, and is still the earliest known. Others have been found at Buscot, Sonning and Sutton Courtenay. The so-called causeway camps, circular ditches with a causewayed entrance, are believed to have been meeting places for a variety of activities: festivals and ceremonial occasions, and trading, and penning cattle. The one at Abingdon has long been known to archaeologists and is of special importance because of its association with a distinctive type of pottery, but other examples, such as one at Eton Wick, have recently been identified by aerial photography.

More impressive as features of the modern landscape, however, are the long barrows in which Neolithic men buried their dead. These became commonplace in southern England in the middle Neolithic period. Berkshire has few compared with the counties to the west, but there are at least six on the chalk hillside overlooking the Vale of the White Horse and others at Blewbury and Inkpen. The oldest is found at Lambourn. The use of turves in its construction suggests that forest clearance had already begun

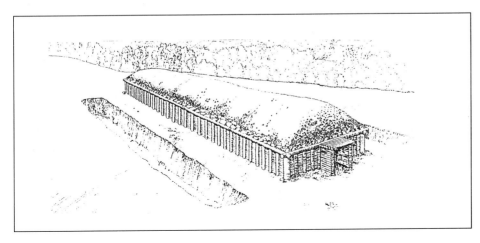

14 *Reconstruction of a long barrow.*

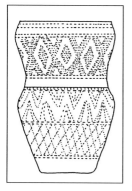

15 *Beaker from one of the Lambourn barrows.*

in this part of the downs when it was built about 3,400 BC. Wayland's Smithy is deservedly the most famous of this type, for it consists of a long barrow, above which is a unique barrow composed of two stone chambers. The delightful legend, which tells of an invisible blacksmith with magical powers which gives the site its name, belongs to a much later period when iron was in use.

On the downlands of the neighbouring counties there is abundant evidence of the importance of the chalk areas to the Neolithic people, for here they built their great monuments known as henges, including the most famous, Stonehenge and Avebury. There are no such henges in Berkshire and no settlement sites on the chalk for this period. There is no easy explanation as to why, but the picture painted by earlier historians of prehistoric man favouring the chalk hills and avoiding the thick oak woods of the Thames Valley is no longer believed to be true.

About 2,300 BC a new group of people began migrating into this country. They have been named the Beaker people after their distinctive shaped clay pots known to archaeologists as 'beakers'. They brought with them a knowledge of working with metal—copper —and they represent a transitional period between the Neolithic and the Bronze Age. Copper was not readily available in southern Britain, and while a few newcomers and enterprising natives obtained metal tools, most families continued to use stone. In general the newcomers were farming people, growing cereals and other crops, keeping cattle, and using their surplus for trade. They buried their dead in round barrows and believed in an after-life; examples of their distinctive pottery 'beakers' are frequently found as grave goods. Several flat, unmarked graves of the Beaker people have also been found at Abingdon. One of them contained a skeleton of a man with a barbed and tanged arrow head jutting out of his spine; his own supply of arrows had been buried with him.

At least thirty-two round barrows lie in close proximity near Lambourn, the so-called Seven Barrows group. Many more are scattered over the Berkshire Downs, singly and in rows, and there are small concentrations in other parts of the county—four at Cookham and three at Radley in the Thames Valley, and others on the poorer soils in the south of the county at Ascot, Bracknell, Finchampstead, Sunninghill, Winkfield, Mortimer, and on Greenham Common and Wash Common at Newbury. Not all of these barrows were built by the Beaker people, for round barrows are also characteristic of the later Bronze Age, and at Abingdon barrows are found in what might be called a 'prehistoric cemetery', for it includes a whole sequence of burials from Neolithic to Saxon.

For many years it was believed that the introduction of bronze weapons and implements around 1,500 BC was brought about by waves of immigrants; those who dominated southern England the archaeologists have named the Wessex Culture. Such ideas are no longer tenable. The replacement of copper by bronze was a gradual process, brought about perhaps by small groups of people, traders and itinerant smiths. Hoards of bronze wares are thought to have been buried for safe keeping or for re-smelting

while customers were sought. Sometimes, as in the case of the 18 implements found at Slough, they were scrap metal, broken items which would
be smelted down and then re-cast. For many people, however, life did not
change much, or only very slowly. Over the centuries, however, regional
differences developed, detected today by changes in styles of pottery and
other possessions. The introduction of metal working and increased trade
also stimulated some important changes in society, such as the emergence
of larger numbers of artisans and craftsmen and an élite which was wealthy
enough to buy luxury goods made of gold, amber and faience (imported
blue beads).

It was for this élite that the large barrows were built. A ceremonial
battle axe and mace-head made from an antler were found in one of the
Lambourn barrows, and gold and amber jewellery in others—clear evidence
of the wealth and warrior status of families who could command sufficient
labour to build these monuments to themselves and their women folk. Their
wealth was almost certainly based on cattle, and the Bronze Age saw the
clearance of more woodland from the Berkshire Downs and the increased
use of them for pasture. An ancient enclosure near the Ridgeway known as
Rams Hill, now only visible from the air, is believed to have been a seasonal
settlement or cattle corral. Extensive linear earthworks known as 'ranch'
boundary ditches (because they may demarcate grazing areas), have been
found; they were constructed during the Middle and Late Bronze Age. The
longest in Berkshire, known as Grims Ditch, runs just north of the Ridgeway
through Ardington, Aston Upthorp and Blewbury for over eight miles—
much too long for it to be a boundary between property or pasture and
arable. Instead it has been suggested that it is a major boundary separating
people of different social groups.

Until relatively recently, very few Bronze-Age settlement sites had been
found, and it was therefore reasoned that the people were nomadic
pastoralists. But recent discoveries have altered our interpretation of the
Bronze Age, although the picture is still far from clear. The sites of numerous farmsteads and small farming communities have been found in the
Thames and Kennet Valleys, and a large farming community at Knights
Farm just south of Reading. There were also farmsteads and small communities living on the chalk lands, such as at Beedon. Pollen analysis of water-
logged material taken from an excavation of a settlement at Pingewood
indicates that here was open country with arable fields, grazing land and
patches of woodland. Elsewhere systems of ditches and banks are evidence
of extensive Bronze-Age field systems, with livestock grazing on the lower,
wetter ground, and cereals grown on the higher gravel terraces. Flax was
also grown for cloth making. At Anslows' Cottages between Reading and
Burghfield the remains of a settlement and a small jetty have been found
alongside an old channel of the Kennet. Here evidence of fish and eel traps
in abandoned channels suggests that fishing was an important occupation.
The large number of bronze tools and weapons recovered from the Thames
and Kennet also points to the general importance of the rivers in the region,

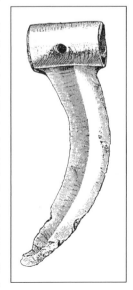

16 *Bronze sickle from
the Thames at Windsor.*

17 *An imaginary scene: a Bronze-Age community.*

and it has been suggested that the riverside settlements found at Bray, Wallingford, and Runnymede in Surrey, were 'high status' settlements. The latter two appear to have been inland ports controlling the river traffic and prospering through the exchange of valuable commodities. At Runnymede the river bank was reinforced by wooden piles to form a substantial waterfront at which boats could be moored. Some very fine quality bronze work and pottery was found at these sites, including antler cheek pieces and bronze fittings which are the earliest indication that horses were being used for riding in the Bronze Age. The enormous quantities of bronze and iron items found in the Thames would appear to be too many to be the result of accidental losses and it seems quite likely that some were votive offerings.

Despite its prosperity Bronze-Age Britain was relatively insular, but from about 750 BC there was increased contact with the Continent and trade in goods. Overseas trade increased dramatically, and with it came the knowledge of working with iron and new ideas for the production of pottery and styles of metalwork; Britain had moved into the Iron Age. No doubt over the centuries many people from the Continent influenced British craftsmen, but they also developed their own styles with many regional variations. By the fourth century BC, if not long before, regional groups had begun to evolve which before the end of the Iron Age would be recognised as tribes and petty kingdoms.

By this date it would also appear that in some areas the increased exploitation of the land and the rising population meant that land became in short supply. Weapons became more common and settlements replaced their enclosure fences with earthworks, signs perhaps that society was becoming more aggressive and that property and territory needed to be defended. Hill forts were now a feature of the landscape, many of them with a series of impressive ramparts and ditches, and space to accommodate a large number of people. It must have required a great number of people and considerable organisation to build them. There are more than twenty hill forts in Berkshire, the largest (with over 80 acres) at Walbury Hill, near Inkpen. Both Segsbury Camp on the downs and Caesar's Camp at Bracknell cover more than twenty acres. Rams Hill was refortified for a short period and then probably abandoned in favour of the more defensible site at Uffington where a hill fort sits at the highest point of the chalk scarp. The forts were probably used for a variety of purposes—corralling cattle, religious or secular meetings, as regional centres, and when the need arose for defence. It may not be simply the accident of preservation that some of the most impressive of the Berkshire hill forts are in the north of the county, for it is here that before the end of the Iron Age three tribes would struggle for supremacy.

2

The Invaders, 150 BC-AD 1066

The Atrebates: Belgic Kingdom and Roman Civitas

During the late second and early first centuries BC, southern Britain was raided and settled by people from the Belgic areas of Gaul. They were part of a widespread movement of people displaced by Roman activities and the westward migrations of people from central to northern Europe. These newcomers to Britain came from different parts of Gaul, and in their new homeland they retained some of their old allegiances. By the mid-first century BC Britain had a large number of tribal areas, some of which might already be called kingdoms. Of these tribal areas, three were important in the history of the area that became Berkshire—the Dobunni, the Atrebates and the Catuvellauni.

Gaul was now part of the Roman Empire, but as yet Rome knew little about Britain though it was rumoured to have rich sources of precious metals. The desire to plunder almost certainly influenced Caesar's decision to invade in 55 BC, although the official reason was to stop aid reaching the Gauls from their kinsmen and allies in Britain. Caesar sent a warship to reconnoitre while he set about getting a fleet of warships ready. News of the coming invasion, however, reached Britain and envoys were sent to Rome to negotiate. Caesar sent them back home accompanied by Commius, king of the Atrebates in Gaul and an ally of Caesar. This, however, proved to be a mistake, for several British tribes joined forces to repel the Romans and Commius was taken prisoner.

Caesar's invasion was initially successful and Commius was handed back to the Romans. But storms damaged their ships and Caesar was forced to seek refuge in Gaul. The following year Caesar again invaded Britain. The campaign of 54 BC was

18 *The tribal areas of late Iron-Age Berkshire.*

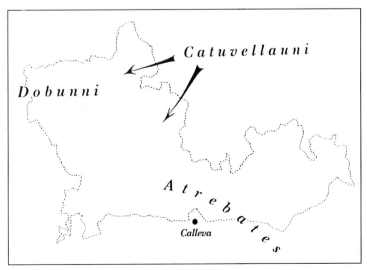

19 *Celtic coin bearing the name of Commius, King of the Atrebates.*

longer and the Roman army penetrated as far inland as Hertfordshire where it defeated the British war leader, Cassivellaunus. Hostages were taken and annual tributes demanded, but then, when success seemed within his grasp, Caesar had to abandon any plans of further victories in order to deal with rebellion in Gaul.

Although Caesar's invasion was an overall failure, the campaigns had succeeded in opening up to Rome the territories of those tribes, such as the Catuvellauni, who had made alliance with Caesar. There was no such trade in wines and other luxuries for those, like the Atrebates, who remained hostile. Meanwhile Commius had changed sides during the Gallic uprising and was forced to flee to Britain where he found refuge with his fellow Atrebates living south of the Thames. Within a short time he had made himself their king and was issuing his own coins—an achievement which attests his strength of leadership and his knowledge of Roman technology. The Belgae had brought to Britain knowledge of the potter's wheel and the use of coins, but those bearing Commius' name are amongst the first inscribed coins to be minted in Britain. The majority of those found come from the Silchester area just south of the present Berkshire boundary. Here, on an easily defended spur of gravel, Commius founded Calleva Atrebatum (Silchester), a name which translated from the Celtic means 'wooded place of the Atrebates'. Exactly what kind of place is not certain, but recent excavations have revealed traces of Iron Age round houses dated from the mid to late first century BC.

Over the next ninety or so years, the Celtic tribes were frequently at war and the evidence from coin finds hints at tribal struggles for power, dynastic upheavals and changes in pro- and anti-Roman feelings. Coins used by the Dobunni tribe have been found in northern Berkshire, some of them depicting a stylised horse, and it is possible that the chalk figure of the White Horse was their tribal emblem and marked a communal meeting place or market area, although the horse itself is now believed to be some 3,000 years old.

About 20 BC Commius was succeeded by his son, Tincommius. Some fifteen years later he became an ally of Rome and around the turn of the century Tincommius was forced to flee to Rome and his brother Eppillus became king. He was so much influenced by the Romans that he styled himself in Latin as REX CALLE, king of Calleva, on his coins. Inter-tribal feuding brought his reign to an end within a few years and Verica then became king. He was probably a grandson of Commius, and by his reign Calleva had been rebuilt. The old round houses had been demolished, new earthwork defences surrounded the settlement, and the place had the look of a planned settlement with rectangular plots and buildings. There is also evidence of imported luxury items such as wine, olive oil, fine pottery, bronze jewellery and metalwork—all the trappings of a petty king growing rich on the tributes of corn, cattle, hides and slaves exacted from his subjects.

Meanwhile the kingdom of the Catuvellauni which lay to the north of the Thames had begun to expand, engulfing part of the territories of several neighbouring tribes, including the northern Dobunni and the Atrebates. For a short time in the twenties AD, the Atrebates were ruled by the brother of the Catuvellaunian king. Verica, however, fought back and regained his throne, only to lose it again about AD 41 to the new king of the Catuvellauni and his brother who took over the kingdoms of the Cantii and the Atrebates. They were both aggressively anti-Roman. Verica fled to Rome in a last ditch attempt to regain his throne, and there appealed to Claudius, the Roman Emperor, for help. Claudius had only recently been made emperor and he needed an opportunity to gain military glory in order to consolidate his own throne. The army he sent to Britain came not to help Verica, but to make Britain part of the Roman Empire.

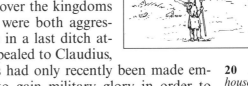

20 *A Celtic round house.*

The army landed in Kent in the summer of AD 43 and by August Claudius had received submissions from several British tribes. Triumphant, he returned to Rome leaving the army to set about making Britain a new Roman province. Responsibility for the conquest of southern Britain was given to the Second Augustan Legion. During the next four years the legion fought 30 battles, but the Atrebates and northern Dobunni offered no opposition; on the contrary, it is likely that they welcomed the Romans because they had defeated their old enemy, the Catuvellauni. By AD 47 a first military frontier had been established in the west, and southern Britain had become a province of Rome. The Atrebates were not strictly part of it, for their territory had become a 'client kingdom'. Finds of military metalwork and the evidence of a large timber building suggest that a unit of the army was encamped at Calleva for the first few years, perhaps to ensure the smooth transfer of administrative power to the new ruler of the kingdom. He was not Verica, but Cogidubnus. Little is known about his earlier life, but whatever services he had performed for Claudius had brought him rich rewards. He later took the name Tiberius Claudius Cogidubnus and became a full Roman citizen. It also seems likely that towards the end of his life he built for himself the palace at Fishbourne in Sussex.

Calleva now became one of the two administrative centres of the new kingdom. The concept of a town and urban life was new to Britain and we do not know how much was achieved at Calleva during this early period, but a new grid-like street plan was laid out and a public bath house built before Cogidubnus' death in AD 80. The town also became an important route centre with metalled roads radiating from its gates in five directions: to Dorchester on Thames and the north, to London, Winchester, Dorchester, and to Gloucester and Bath. For soldiers, merchants and couriers on imperial service, and those journeying on pilgrimages or holidaying in Bath, Calleva was the natural overnight stop.

The countryside had long been criss-crossed by a network of tracks and footpaths, but these Roman roads were unlike anything ever seen in Britain before. They were built by army engineers to facilitate the movement of soldiers and the baggage trains carrying food and equipment. The

21 *Roman Berkshire showing the known Roman roads.*

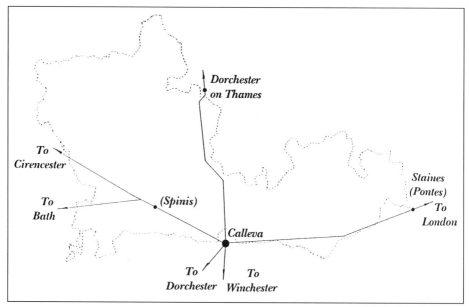

roads, however, were soon more important as trade and communication routes than for military purposes. Built on wide embankments known as *aggers*, these roads were an imposing new feature of the landscape. Their metalled and cambered surfaces were a striking contrast to the native roads which had been formed simply by the feet of men and livestock.

After the death of Cogidubnus, his kingdom was dissolved and split into three parts, each of which was a *civitas*, a self-governing district of non-Roman citizens within the Roman Province. The most northerly was Civitas Atrebatum with a territory which covered the whole of pre-1974 Berkshire and adjacent parts of Wiltshire and Hampshire. Calleva as its administrative capital soon gained several public buildings. In the centre were the forum, basilica and piazza, the three main civic buildings of any Roman town. Here the council met, public meetings were held and the law administered. The first-century public buildings were built of timber; they were replaced by imposing stone in the middle of the second century. The town also had several temples, two bath houses, an amphitheatre and an inn for the use of the *cursus publicus*, or official courier service. There were also at least sixteen large courtyard houses, as well as many smaller houses which also had mosaic floors, painted walls and courtyards. The main shopping area would appear to have been the east-west street to the north of the forum, but evidence of industrial activities has been found in many other parts of the town. These include a tannery, silversmith's, bronze and blacksmiths' and coopers' workshops.

Calleva was the only large town within Civitas Atrebatum, but an official itinerary, drawn up in the second century when Antonius was emperor, lists 'Spinis' as a staging post between Calleva and Cunetio (at Marlborough), the

next town on the Roman road to Bath and Gloucester. The site of Spinis has not been discovered, but it lay to the west of Newbury, somewhere near one of the two villages which have inherited its name—Speen and Woodspeen. Like Calleva, Spinis would have been expected to provide accommodation where couriers, highway inspectors, and tax collectors could find refreshment, a change of horses and perhaps a bed for the night.

22 Aerial view of Silchester showing the outline of the Roman town as crop marks.

Outside the towns the wealthy lived in villas, the landed estates of the Romanised inhabitants. The houses at the centre of the estates were undoubtedly impressive buildings, built of brick or stone, with tiled roofs, several rooms, painted walls, mosaic courtyards, hypocausts and baths. One of the most fully excavated Berkshire villas now lies under a housing estate at Cox Green near Maidenhead. It was built in the second century as a relatively modest 'corridor villa' with only two rooms; it was enlarged in several phases until there were 18 rooms at its greatest extent in the late fourth century. There were three similar villas at Cranhill in the parish of Letcombe Regis, Eling in the parish of Hampstead Norris, and Frilford, and others at West Challow, Kingston Lisle, Woolstone, and

23 An imaginary view of the Cox Green Roman villa, Maidenhead.

24 *Roman temple at Weycock Hill.*

Barton Court. There is evidence of other stone-built houses in Berkshire, but no rich early Roman villas as in neighbouring areas have yet been discovered. This was probably because Civitas Atrebatum was originally a client kingdom whose king lived on the south coast.

As well as the villas and Romanised towns, there was a wide range of Romano-British habitation sites. Some, like the large settlement on the western side of modern Thatcham, were roadside villages, but this village was rather more than that, for its inhabitants were engaged in smelting and the manufacture of items from iron, bronze, and clay, using wood, peat and coal for fuel. Finds of hippo-sandals, the over-shoes worn by horses carrying heavy loads over steep or frozen ground, point to an all-year-round movement of carts and pack horses into the village. Not far away at Colthrop, where the Roman road crosses the Kennet Valley, one carrier ran off the road, and he and his horse and cart were swallowed up in the adjacent marsh. In 1921 workmen digging for gravel found the two skeletons and one of the cart wheels.

There was a small industrial town at Wickham Bushes near the Roman Road through present-day Easthamstead, and substantial villages have been located at Abingdon and near Weycock Hill where an octagonal temple was excavated in the 19th century. Another temple was found at Frilford, close to a junction of two roads on the site of an Iron-Age shrine; both may have been local religious centres. Excavations and aerial photography have located farmsteads at Knowl Hill and Finchampstead adjacent to the Roman road. The great majority of the rural population lived in farmsteads and small hamlets which owed little to Roman influence. The principal structure was still the round house which was used as a dwelling, as a workshop, and for sheltering the livestock. They were often surrounded by rectangular ditches and banks, and many farmhouses and homesteads, such as those at Ufton Nervet, Theale Green and Long Wittenham, appear to have been continuously occupied from Belgic into Roman times. The pattern of rural settlement is densest on the river gravels and the chalk platform between Maidenhead and Wargrave, where there are traces of an occupation site every two square miles. There are fewer sites on the London Clay, the Bagshot Beds and the chalk downs, but it is likely that these areas were farmed, though less intensely. An extensive area of Roman arable fields has been found at Maddle Farm at the head of the Lambourn Valley.

The period of Roman rule lasted almost four hundred years, and inevitably important changes took place during that time. Christianity was added to the list of religions practised in Britain; a church was built near the west gate of Calleva sometime during the fourth century. A font with Christian symbols has been found at Caversham and a Christian cemetery at Newbury. New earthwork defences were built in the second century in response to dissension within the empire, and these were replaced a hundred years later by a three-metre-thick stone wall. It has been estimated that this would have entailed carrying over a hundred-thousand wagon

I *Reading town hall, a splendid Victorian building recently renovated.*

II *The old county hall, Abingdon on Thames.*

III *The ancient boundary of Windsor Great Park is marked today by a line of trees and a slight bank to the east of the main road through the park. Today the land on the other side of the road also belongs to the Great Park, but in earlier centuries it lay within the privately owned Moat Park.*

IV *Diorama of the market at Windsor based on John Norden's map of 1607. Notice the market house built in 1592 and the old parish church in the background.*

loads of flint and more than forty-thousand loads of bonding stones—a mammoth undertaking which must surely have taken several years. In every part of Roman Britain and the western empire, cities were being provided with new strong defences because of the unrest on the frontiers.

By the late fourth century the Roman Empire was in decline. Archaeological evidence suggests that many large towns in Britain, including Calleva, suffered from a recession. There was little rebuilding or refurbishment, and maintenance work on the public baths and sewage systems was neglected with unpleasant results. At Calleva, the basilica was no longer used for civic purposes; instead the premises were taken over for industrial purposes. No new villas were built, nor were there any extensions to existing ones.

In AD 402 the last issue of bronze coins was sent to Britain from Rome; no coins of any kind were supplied after 411. Many were hoarded, some—like those found at Matthews Green, Wokingham and at Kimber Farm, Oakley Green—never to be used again. In 407 the Roman army (under the British emperor, Constantine III) left Britain to fight in Gaul, never to return. In 410 the Emperor Honorius wrote to the cities of Britain telling them to defend themselves. Britain had ceased to be part of the Roman Empire.

Within a generation many Roman towns in Britain had ceased to function as urban centres; everywhere urban life was breaking down and with it Roman society. The reasons for this are complex. The removal of central government and the loss of the army and the decline of cities as major markets for produce and manufactured goods, the end of tax collection and the disappearance of a money-based economy are seen by some historians as crucial factors, unrelated to the incursion by new invaders who certainly also played a part in the destruction of Romanised society. Internecine fighting and the neglect of roads and bridges further weakened the functions of the towns, and plagues and famine added to their downfall. The citizens of Calleva appear to have attempted to defend the town, and the community would seem to have managed to survive for three or four generations, but by the mid-sixth century the site was virtually abandoned.

In the countryside, the inhabitants fared only a little better, and farmstead and hamlets reverted to a mainly subsistence economy. Bridges which were not repaired collapsed, and unmaintained road surfaces deteriorated under the attack of weather and vegetation. With the loss of the bridge across the Thames at Pontes (Staines) and no major town at Calleva, the great Roman road west across Berkshire no longer had a purpose and fell out of use.

The century after the Romans left was a terrible period, neither Roman Britain, nor yet Saxon England. It was a dangerous time to live, but one which also gave birth to one of our best loved legends, that of King Arthur defending Britain against the invading Saxons. But of the part played by Berkshire in these struggles, the records are silent.

Saxon Berrocshire: The Coming of the Saxons

Unlike the Roman legions, the Anglo-Saxons did not come to Britain as soldiers in the pay of a mighty empire but as small groups of men intent on taking what they could in riches and land. They came at first as raiders or as mercenaries hired by a British leader to fight against other Saxons. No one decisive event comparable with the Roman invasion marked their coming, and it took almost two hundred years before Roman Britain could be called Saxon England.

Our knowledge of these early years comes from three main sources—archaeological excavations, the interpretation of place names, and oral traditions as recorded later by Gildas, Bede and the authors of the Anglo Saxon Chronicle. The evidence is fragmentary, difficult to interpret and conflicting, but something of the story of the colonisation of the area known as Berkshire and its formation as an administrative unit known as *Berrocshire* can be pieced together—though not all historians tell the same story!

The story begins in the Upper Thames Valley where archaeological evidence has been found of Germanic, or Saxon, people living there before the Roman army left Britain. They are thought to have been mercenaries employed to defend the northern boundaries of the Atrebates territory from Saxon invaders. Although presumably dependant upon the nearby Roman town of Dorchester on Thames, and ultimately upon Calleva, the soldiers would appear to have been stationed in various British villages. According to Gildas, describing events about AD 430 in an unnamed part of Britain, when supplies and money ran out the mercenaries devastated with fire cities and lands 'until it [the fire] burnt nearly the whole surface of the islands, and licked the western Ocean with its red and savage tongue'. There is no evidence of any such devastation at Dorchester or Calleva, but by the mid-fifth century the situation had changed: the mercenaries had become farmers and had been joined by waves of new settlers.

25 *Early Saxon brooch and buckle.*

We do not know why these people chose to settle here, so far inland, or by what route they came, though finds of distinctive types of urns and brooches suggest that some had earlier settled in eastern Britain and made their way to the Upper Thames along the ancient track known as the Icknield Way. Others came from the south east, following the Thames Valley. Early Saxon buildings and other habitation features have been uncovered at Abingdon, Sutton Courtenay, Dorchester and several other places in nearby Oxfordshire. Anglo-Saxon cemeteries which were in use over several generations have been found on both sides of the Thames, including East Shefford, Long Wittenham, Reading, Wallingford and Aston in Berkshire. A remarkable concentration of topographical names suggests that the Saxons had soon expanded into the fertile valley of the Ock, establishing villages there with names which testify to the importance of rivers and streams to these farming people. This Upper Thames Valley region was perhaps the most important of the inland areas of early Saxon colonisation, and the emergence of Wessex, the greatest of all the Saxon kingdoms.

Numerous battles took place between Britons and Saxons in the turbulent years of the fifth and sixth centuries. Although none is known to have taken place in the region which was to become Berkshire, the Anglo Saxon Chronicle tells the story of two men, Cerdic and Cynric, war lords who landed on the coast in Hampshire and who made their way inland by a series of battles. It was they who, according to tradition, welded the settlers in the Upper Thames Valley into a kingdom and in the early years of the sixth century founded the royal house of Wessex.

The Formation of the Shire

For much of the fifth century southern Berkshire (the area which in 1995, more or less, constituted the county) was still occupied mainly by Britons, and Calleva Atrebatum functioned as a town. Earthworks were constructed which blocked the roads leading northwards to Dorchester, perhaps in an attempt to prevent the expansion of the Saxons. But the tide of new settlers could not be stopped. Many Britons fled westwards to Wales and Cornwall or northwards to find refuge in less favourable areas such as the Chilterns. Calleva Atrebatum was finally abandoned sometime in the sixth century and the rest of the old Roman province of the Atrebates was gradually colonised by the Saxons. Topographical place names and those containing the Saxon word 'ham', meaning village, or 'ingas' or 'ingham', which incorporates a word meaning people, indicate some of the areas which were relatively early settled. The Britons who remained learned to co-exist with the newcomers, passing on their names for the hills and rivers and some of their villages. The names Thames, Kennet and Loddon are all names derived from the British, or Celtic, language: Datchet, Pinge, Altwood (in Maidenhead) and Crutchfield in Bray are also at least partly British. There is also a sprinkling of names which are thought to have a Latin origin, such as Speen which apparently comes from the Roman town of Spinis. The Latin word for a small town, *vicus*, gave rise to two place names not far from Roman roads, Wickham in the parish of Welford and Wickham Bushes, an area of heathland on the line of the Roman road in Easthampstead parish. There are a few other names. The most intriguing survival from these centuries is the legend of Herne the Hunter, who it is believed was the Celtic god, Cernunnos. Shakespeare immortalised him in *The Merry Wives of Windsor* with Sir John Falstaff meeting the merry wives under Herne's oak.

The final conquest of the midlands and southern Britain by the Saxons took place in the second half of the sixth century. By the end of the century the kingdom of Wessex encompassed the whole of northern and western Berkshire and extended as far south as Devon. Britain, the land of the Britons, had now become England, but it was not one country, but a conglomeration of rival Anglo-Saxon kingdoms. The most important for the history of Berkshire were Wessex, Mercia, and Essex with its subsidiary 'districts' of Middlesex and Surrey.

26 *Drinking horn from the Taplow tumuli, the burial mound of a rich Saxon who died about AD 620.*

At this date the Upper Thames basin would appear to have been at the heart of Wessex for here, at Dorchester on Thames, Birinius was established as the first bishop of Wessex in 634, just two years after he had converted Cynegils, King of Wessex, to Christianity. The Anglo Saxon Chronicle records that Birinius had been sent by Pope Honorarius, but little else. There is a tradition, however, that the King's baptism took place at Taplow, just across the present county boundary, by a pool that has been known as Bapsey Pond for many years. The truth of this legend we may never know, but in the seventh century Taplow was a place of some importance, for only some yards away to the north is the pagan burial mound of a very rich Saxon who gave his name to the village—Tappa's *hlaw*.

As yet there was no such place as Berkshire, nor an administrative unit with a different name which covered more or less the same area. During the seventh and eighth centuries northern and western Berkshire was disputed territory between the kingdoms of Wessex and Mercia. Mercia had begun as a small kingdom near the River Trent, which under King Penda, a powerful ruler, expanded to cover the greater part of the Midlands. In 643 King Cynegils of Wessex died and was succeeded by his son Cenwalh who married one of Penda's sisters. When Cenwalh repudiated her, Penda invaded Wessex and Cenwalh was forced to flee. On his return three years later, he made a grant to a kinsman of '3,000 hides of land by Ashdown'. Historians are agreed that this was an unusually large tract of land for such a gift and have argued that it established a frontier province to act as a bulwark against further Mercian hostilities. Ashdown was the old name for the Berkshire Downs and 3,000 hides was large enough to have included the whole of northern and western Berkshire. A few years later Cenwalh moved the seat of the Wessex bishopric from Dorchester on Thames to a safer location at Winchester. Soon after his death, the Wessex territory north of the Thames was taken into Mercia.

Eastern Berkshire was not part of this frontier province. It was not within either Wessex or Mercia, but was part of the neighbouring kingdom of Middlesex. In the early years of the Saxon invasion, Middlesex encompassed London and a southern region—Surrey. Place-name evidence suggests that this southern region included the middle Thames Valley of present-day eastern Berkshire, north and south of the Thames, with the sparsely populated wooded area (later known as Windsor Forest) forming its western boundary. By the seventh century, however, Middlesex had been absorbed into the more powerful kingdom of Essex. In 672-4 the overlordship of Surrey, however, was claimed by Mercia, and a grant by its sub-king refers to a province called Sonning after a tribal group who gave their name not only to the village of Sonning, but also to Sunninghill and Sunningdale on the Berkshire/Surrey boundary. Wokingham, a town once part of Sonning parish, also had Surrey connections for it was probably settled by people from Woking.

The frontier province of northern and western Berkshire was now governed by a sub-king named Cissa who, in 675, gave 20 hides near

Time Chart II

Some important dates during the periods of invasion

c.150 BC	onwards Belgic people (Iron Age) moving into Britain
55 BC	1st Roman invasion
43 AD	2nd Roman invasion
410	End of the Roman province of Britain
634	Cynegils, King of Wessex converted to Christianity
643	Penda, King of Mercia invades Wessex
646	Formation of a frontier province of 3,000 hides
646	Berkshire men fighting the Vikings
860	Earliest record of the county name
871	Danes invade Berkshire for first time
878	Division of England into Saxon and Danish territories
994	First payment of danegeld by Berkshire
1066	The Norman Conquest

The changing overlordship of the northern frontier or buffer zone which later became known as Berkshire

Part of Wessex	Part of Mercia	Decisive events which changed the overlordship of Berkshire
c.516-634		Wessex Founded by Cerdic
	643-646	King Penda of Mercia invaded Wessex
646-726		Cenealh established frontier province
	726-757	Aethelbald of Mercia became dominant king
757-799		King Cynwulf of Wessex retook the area
	799-829	King Offa of Mercia defeats Cynwulf
829-830		King Egbert of Wessex defeated the Mercian army
	830-c.844	King of Mercia regained his kingdom
844-1066		King Aethelwulf of Wessex took the province in exchange for help given to King Beorhtwulf of Mercia

Abingdon to his nephew Hean, on condition that he built an abbey on the land. Little transpired for several years, but eventually, after King Ine of Wessex had made further grants of land, an abbey was built at Abingdon sometime before 699. In 709 Hean entered the religious life and became its first abbot.

After Ine's abdication in 726, the fortunes of war once again swung against Wessex, and Aethelbald of Mercia became the dominant king in southern England. There is little evidence of battles taking place in 'Berkshire', but the chronicle of Abingdon Abbey shows that during this period the monks regarded King Aethelbald as their protector, and in 731 he gave a monastery at Cookham to the Archbishop of Canterbury. Little is known about this religious house, the only known Saxon monastery in the Sonning province of eastern Berkshire. We have no date for its foundation, and, although it was important enough to be the venue of a synod in the eighth century, it did not survive the Danish invasions.

The records of these two abbeys would seem to suggest that both parts of Berkshire—the old buffer zone of the north and west, and Sonning province—were once again under the rule of Mercia, but only for a few years. They were recaptured during the early years of the reign of Cynewulf of Wessex (757-788), only to be taken again by King Offa of Mercia in 799. The chronicle of Abingdon Abbey records that Offa added to his rule all the country from the Icknield Way and the Thames, from Wallingford to Ashdown. A charter tells us that Offa also took the monastery at Cookham and other towns from Cynewulf and added them to Mercia.

Offa of Mercia campaigned against every part of Britain, extending his influence over the whole of England south of the Humber. Not all of the rival kingdoms became part of Mercia, although they paid tribute to him. Mercia itself was divided into provinces governed by ealdormen. Almost certainly the 'Berkshire' buffer zone formed one of these provinces, and it may not have mattered too much to its inhabitants in which kingdom they lived. More important were the character of the ealdorman and the amount of taxes that was demanded by him.

Berkshire remained part of Mercia for some fifty years through the reigns of Cenwulf and Ceolwulf. In 823 Ceolwulf was deposed, and with him the dynasty which had given Mercia its supremacy came to an end. Wessex was now ruled by Egbert, and in 825 he met and defeated the Mercian army at Wroughton, near Swindon. The men of Surrey (including one might presume the province of Sonning), Sussex and Essex submitted to Egbert because, according to the Anglo Saxon Chronicle, 'they had been wrongly forced from their loyalty to his kinsmen'. In 829 Egbert conquered Mercia; both parts of 'Berkshire' were now part of Wessex. But within a year the king of Mercia had regained his kingdom, and a grant made in 844 by the Bishop of Leicester to Beorhtwulf of Mercia of an estate at Pangbourne in exchange for several monasteries, including Abingdon, suggests that northern and western 'Berkshire' (if not the whole 'county') now belonged to Mercia and was part of the Mercian diocese of Leicester. Almost immediately Beorhtwulf gave the Pangbourne estate to the ealdorman named Aethelwulf who governed the buffer province.

27 *Silver penny bearing the names of King Beohrtwulf of Mercia and King Aethelwulf of Wessex.*

Sometime after this the province was recovered by Egbert's son, King Aethelwulf of Wessex. Five years later, however, it was still being governed by the Mercian ealdorman. Perhaps he had changed loyalties, but it is more likely that this time the transfer of Berkshire from Mercia to Wessex was not accomplished by fighting but by negotiated exchange. Mercia had requested help from Wessex in the fight against their common enemy—the Vikings; Berkshire was perhaps the price paid by Mercia. A unique coin with the name Beorhtwulf of Mercia on one side and that of Ethelwulf of Wessex on the other, may commemorate this event. In 849 Prince Alfred, Ethelwulf's fourth son, was born at Wantage, a royal estate, and in 853 a marriage between the royal households cemented the alliance between Wessex and Mercia.

Both parts of Berkshire—the ancient buffer zone of northern and western Berkshire and the Sonning Province of eastern Berkshire—were now within Wessex, but how and when the two parts became one shire and the Sonning province separated from Surrey is uncertain. The only clues come from the place names and the relationship of an old Roman road to the county and parish boundaries. The juxtaposition of eight parishes all with names ending in feld (meaning open land)— Arborfield, Bradfield, Burghfield, Englefield, Shinfield, Stratfield, Swallowfield and Wokefield— suggests the existence of a belt of heathland on the edge of Windsor Forest.

28   The statue of King Alfred at Wantage unveiled by the Prince of Wales in 1877.

Within the area of the ancient forest there are other *feld* names (such as Binfield), and several place names which incorporate the word *legh* (meaning a woodland clearing) and *hyrst* (meaning a wood). Such a concentration of these types of names suggests that this area was colonised long after the rest of the county, perhaps in the late Saxon period. Until this took place, any boundary between the Sonning Province and the rest of Surrey would have been ill-defined. However, although long out of use, the old Roman road (now known as the Devil's Highway) was still a prominent feature and a convenient one which could be used as a boundary when at last the province was detached from Surrey. Today the county boundary follows the old highway for several miles.

29   Ninth-century Berkshire.

It seems likely that at about the same time the two parts became one shire it took on a new name— Berrocshire. The earliest record of the name occurs in 860. Berkshire appears to have become a shire long after the rest of Wessex and the choice of name is a strange one, for it relates neither to a group of people nor to the most important town, as do most of the other shires. Instead, according to Asser, a Welsh monk who wrote a biography of King Alfred, it is called after the Berroc Wood, a Celtic name which commemorated the abundance of trees. Rather surprisingly, the wood was not

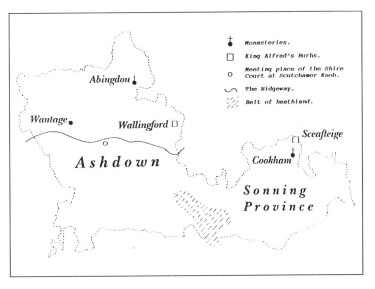

in the northern part of the county, the heart of the ancient buffer zone, but in the south west of the county and many miles from the meeting place of the shire court, a mound known as Scutchamer Knob in the parish of East Hendred, high up on the Berkshire Downs.

The Viking Invasion

Scandinavian raiders began plundering coastal settlements of Britain in the late eighth century, but until the 830s such raids were infrequent. In 835 Danish Vikings overran the Isle of Sheppey at the mouth of the Thames, and from then on for many decades they were an ever-present and terrifying threat. Responsibility for local defence rested on the ealdormen of each threatened shire. The first known contact with this region took place in 860 when a 'great host landed and stormed Winchester', and the men of Berkshire joined with men from Hampshire and fought together under their respective ealdormen, Ethelwulf and Osric.

Five years later, a huge army under several Danish kings and earls landed in East Anglia. This time the Danes came not merely to raid and return home but to stay—to seize defendable sites, to fortify them, and then systematically to ravage the countryside until its inhabitants were willing to pay for peace. In 871 the Danes marched into Wessex and set up camp at Reading, on the east side of the Saxon settlement. Three days after their arrival they sent out a raiding party led by two earls. At Englefield they were met and defeated by Saxons led by ealdorman Ethelwulf. A few days later the West Saxon army attacked the Danish camp but with disastrous results; they were defeated and ealdorman Ethelwulf was amongst those killed.

Four days later the two armies met on Ashdown, the ancient name for the Berkshire Downs. Although the Danes had the higher position on the hillside, it was the Saxons who won the day under the leadership of King Aethelred and his young brother Alfred. One Danish king, five earls and many other Vikings were slain, their bodies scattered far and wide 'over the whole broad expanse of Ashdown'. The remnants of the Danish army fled back to their stronghold at Reading where they were reinforced by a great 'summer army' from Scandinavia led by Guthrum. The Danes fought and defeated the West Saxons in seven more battles and numerous skirmishes. Abingdon Abbey was destroyed, the Saxon army depleted and King Aethelred died. His younger brother Alfred became king and was forced to buy peace— and time.

Well satisfied, perhaps, the Danes left Reading the following year to plunder and fight elsewhere. By 877 the other Saxon kingdoms of Mercia, East Anglia and Northumbria had all been defeated by the Danes. In the winter of 878 King Guthrum led his army into Wessex and Alfred fled to the Isle of Athelney. The story of Alfred's guerrilla tactics and eventual success at the battle of Edington and the treaty which divided the country into Saxon and Danish territories lies outside the story of Berkshire. But Alfred's dramatic reversal of events ensured the survival of Wessex as a Saxon kingdom and Berkshire as a Saxon shire. It was no longer a frontier district.

Peace, however, needed to be maintained and Alfred now initiated the construction of a series of fortresses, known as burhs, at strategic points throughout Wessex. Two were in Berkshire, at Wallingford and a place named Sceafteige. The Wallingford fortifications consisted of a hundred-acre enclosure surrounded by a high bank and ditch. Sceafteige was built on an island in the Thames at Cookham, known today as Sashes. Like Wallingford it was probably chosen to give command of movement along the Thames and to guard an important road crossing, be it ford, ferry or bridge. No archaeological evidence has yet been found to prove where the Thames was crossed in this stretch of the river before Maidenhead existed, but the circumstantial evidence of a monastery, burh and late Saxon market suggests it might well have been at Cookham.

Arrangements for the repair and manning of the burhs by the men from villages in the surrounding districts are given in a document known as the Burghal Hidage. According to this, in time of danger four men were needed to hold each perch (16.5 feet) of wall, and each village was expected to provide one man for every hide [a measurement of land used for tax purposes] for which it was assessed.

During the next hundred years, hostilities continued intermittently though little is known of events in Berkshire until Viking sea raids began again towards the end of the tenth century. In 994 the first of the danegeld payments—£16,000 on this occasion—was paid to gain a temporary peace. In the winter of 1006 an invading Danish army set out on a raid across Hampshire and Berkshire to Reading, and then north to Wallingford where they set fire to the town. The Danes then struck westwards along the line of the downs, defiantly halting at the shire's meeting place, and then onwards to Winchester and back to their ships. Berkshire was invaded again in 1009 and 1010; in 1011 the Danes overran most of Wessex including Berkshire. By 1013 Swein had become the first of the Danish kings of England. His reign was very short, but his son Cnut (or Canute) reigned for 25 years and brought Danish and Saxon England under one rule. It was a period of peace, albeit one of a conquered country. Danish men who had followed their king were awarded with Saxon lands. Tovi the Proud was granted an estate at Reading.

Towns and villages, estates and parishes

Six centuries of raiding and colonisation by Saxons and Danes had wrought great changes on the landscape, the patterns of settlement and the organisation of the people and government. Although the broad outline of these changes is known, evidence for the detailed picture is hard to find. The names of Berkshire's parishes and towns are almost all Saxon, yet no more than a handful are mentioned in documents written before the Norman Conquest or have produced archaeological evidence of their Saxon beginnings. The Saxons were not town dwellers and only slowly did some villages become towns, by stages which are not yet fully understood. How many towns there were in 10th century Berkshire is a matter of conjecture.

30 *A bronze ornament, usually referred to as the Kingsbury beast, found at Old Windsor.*

More than a dozen places would appear to have possessed some of the attributes which together made a settlement a town rather than a village. Some, like Kintbury, Thatcham and Lambourne, were administrative and judicial centres for divisions of the shire known as Hundreds. Royal estates were also often centres because of the king's use of the place and his encouragement of trade. There were a considerable number of royal estates, including Wantage, Cookham, and Sutton Courtenay; the king's council, or Witan, met at these in 995, 997 and 1042 respectively. It also met at Abingdon in 989, and here King Athelstan held court. There were also religious centres: monasteries and minster churches which served an area known as a *parochiae*. The word has come to mean parish, but in Saxon England it covered a much larger area where as yet there might not be other churches but only preaching crosses. Research suggests that Abingdon, Cookham, Kintbury, Lambourne, Reading, Thatcham and Waltham were all minster churches. Only after estate owners had built churches for their villages could parishes be formed, each with its incumbent responsible for the spiritual care of its parishioners. There was a quickening of religious interest in the 10th century, Abingdon Abbey was rebuilt, and it is likely that many parish churches were built at this time, though few Saxon buildings survive. Occasionally traces of the church have been found, and in a few instances, such as St Swithun's of Wickham, the 10th-century church still serves its parish. At Old Windsor, a royal estate, the original church was used for the consecration of the abbot of St Augustine's of Canterbury in 1061.

By the mid-11th century, at least twenty Berkshire settlements were centres of some kind, but only two would appear to have become fully fledged towns—Wallingford and Reading. Wallingford was situated, as its name implies, at a crossing of the Thames. It was the second largest burh in Wessex and the grid-plan of its oldest streets may date from the construction of the fortification. By the 10th century it had a mint and a market though evidence for the latter is meagre. It was a free borough, the only one in Berkshire in the 10th century. Reading was much smaller and probably later in development; there is no evidence of a mint before 1040. It has no burh, except for the Danish fortifications. It was a royal vill, and the presence of the mint suggests the development of a market and other trading functions.

The pattern of settlement which grew during the Saxon period appears to bear little relationship with that of the Roman province, but many historians are convinced that there was at least some continuity of field and estate boundaries, even though villas and towns were destroyed. Sometime in the late Saxon period, farming practices began to change and the numerous small fields began to be replaced by a lesser number of large fields that were divided into un-hedged strips of land worked by the people of the village. These large fields, which became such a distinctive feature of the countryside, almost certainly came into being as a result of the community working together to enlarge their arable land. There was still much land— forest, heath and marsh—that was unused and not all parish boundaries

were clearly defined. Estates did not
always match with parishes or the field
systems worked by the villages; large
units had been divided and new systems imposed on old. The bounds of
the older Saxon land holdings, however, have sometimes been preserved
as parish boundaries. Pioneer research
in this field has been carried out in
Shellingford, Blewbury and the

31 *Excavation of a
Saxon watermill at Old
Windsor. The mill, built
in the early ninth century,
originally had three
horizontal water wheels,
and is likely to have served
several villages.*

Uffington area. Uffington and the adjacent parish of Woolstone were once
part of a Saxon land unit known as Aescesbyrig (from the nearby hill fort)
which was divided in the second half of the 10th century, the two parts
being named after the new owners—Uffa and Wulfric. There were thus
many local changes during these centuries. But the Norman Conquest in
the mid-11th century brought the greatest change of land ownership since
the Roman invasion a thousand years before.

3

Norman and Medieval Berkshire, 1066-1485

Conquest by the Normans

The Battle of Hastings was only the beginning of William, Duke of Normandy's conquest of England, but there, on the battlefield, Berkshire felt its first losses with the death of Berkshire men who fought in King Harold's army. We do not know the names of most of them, but Abingdon Abbey provided 12 men to fight for Harold, and amongst those who died on that October day in 1066 were Turkville of Kingston Bagpuise and Godric of Fyfield, military tenants of the abbey. Godric was also sheriff of Berkshire, a post which had replaced that of ealdorman.

From Hastings, William marched his victorious army in a wide sweeping curve westwards through southern England to Winchester, the ancient capital of Wessex and residence of Queen Edith, widow of Edward the Confessor. After the surrender of Winchester, the army appears to have divided into three contingents. The main body crossed the River Kennet near Newbury, then marched northwards towards Wantage and finally east to Wallingford where Archbishop Stigand and Wigod of Wallingford (Sheriff of Oxford) swore fealty to William. Another section of the army took a route through Great Shefford and the Lambourn valley, while the third travelled along the Wiltshire/Berkshire border before sweeping east through the Vale of the White Horse. For the people of Berkshire it was a terrifying time. An army must live off the country through which it passes, and William's left a swathe of destruction, the effects of which lasted for more than a generation. But the march accomplished its purpose—the surrender of London—and, 10 weeks after the Battle of Hastings, William was crowned King of England in Westminster Abbey on Christmas Day 1066.

William's followers were awarded with land, the estates of the defeated English landowners, and everywhere the Norman presence was felt as they took over their new estates and became the lords of the manor. Wigod's daughter married Robert D'Oyley, one of William's right-hand men, and he was entrusted with the task of building a castle at Wallingford; it was one of several built during William's first few months in England to ensure the continued loyalty of his conquered subjects. The timber and earthen castle, built no doubt with Saxon labour, occupied the north-east corner of Alfred's

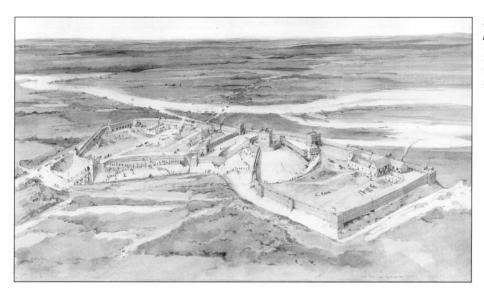

32 *Windsor Castle as it probably looked about 1080 when the walls, tower and other buildings were constructed of timber.*

burh. Little now remains except the artificial mound, or motte, on which the keep stood, a reminder not only of William's military strategy but of the importance of Wallingford. During the civil war when King Stephen and Matilda fought for the English throne, the castle withstood the force of Stephen's army in 1139 and again in 1141 when Matilda sought refuge in the castle after escaping from imprisonment at Oxford.

Unlike burhs, which were for the defence of the town and surrounding area, William's castles were built for his protection, and housed a garrison to over-awe the populace and to deter rebellion. Within a few years of the conquest he had set about building another castle in Berkshire, one of a ring of fortresses round London, each a day's march from the City and the Tower of London. The site chosen was a steep chalk hill, 'the one strong point between London and Wallingford where a fortress could be placed to guard' the Thames valley. This was Windsor Castle, but unlike Wallingford the castle was not built within the town, for Saxon Windsor lay two miles downstream. It was there at 'Old' Windsor that William resided when he visited Berkshire to enjoy hunting in Windsor Forest. The steep hill belonged to the neighbouring manor of Clewer, a name which means 'dwellers by the cliff'. Not until 1110 in the reign of Henry I was the castle used as a palace as well as a fort and prison. At Whitsuntide that year, according to the Anglo Saxon Chronicle, the king 'held his court for the first time at New Windsor'.

Although these early castles were built of timber, the Normans were used to building in stone, and the oldest

33 *The church of St James, Finchampstead showing its rounded chancel apse, a feature of many Norman churches.*

building in present-day Windsor is not the castle but the parish church at Clewer, built of chalk and flints quarried from the castle hill. All over the country, Norman lords replaced Saxon wooden buildings with new stone churches, through a sense of piety or to enjoy the benefit such patronage could bring in terms of prestige and income from offerings and tithes. The evidence is too meagre to document this story in any detail, but by the end of William's reign at least 57 parishes in the county had a church, for they are mentioned in Domesday Book. Even today more than eighty churches display evidence of Norman influence, their distinctive semi-circular arches with zigzag decorations making their Norman origin easy to recognise. The churches at Avington, North Hinksey, Thatcham, Tidmarsh, and Upton (in Slough) all have Norman decorated doorways.

William reigned 19 years before he instituted the survey for which he is famous—Domesday Book. It was compiled at his orders, given to his Council at Christmas 1085; he wanted an up-to-date account of how much

34 *Norman architectural details on Avington church.*

land he held, what it was worth, what he might expect in revenues from his boroughs and shires, and what taxes he might reasonably impose on his tenants-in-chief. Almost immediately men of the highest ranks were appointed as commissioners to supervise the collection of the necessary information from the shires and to pass judgement when there were conflicts of evidence. It was an astonishing undertaking, involving the shire courts where the commissioners presided, and testimonies were taken from those who held land in the shire, as well as from the hundred courts attended by the priest, reeve and six villeins from each village. The information was collated according to the holdings of the tenants-in chief before being abstracted to form a concise report for the Treasury. William's death in September 1087 brought an end to the work before the written report had been completed, but the resultant documents—Domesday Books—give us our first real glimpse of the population and pattern of settlement in Berkshire.

A. *Form & dimensions of the Arch between the Nave and Chancel.*

B.C. *Capitals of the Pillars & part of the Arch of the Door of the Nave.*

D. *Elevation of part of the Arch between the Nave and Chancel.*

Almost two hundred places are mentioned in the Berkshire folios, and there are ten or so others given in the Buckinghamshire, Hampshire,

Oxfordshire and Wiltshire sections, relating to places which were later regarded as being in Berkshire. The true number of villages and hamlets, however, was much greater, for the names recorded were those of the manors, not the settlements. The large manor of Sonning, held in 1086 by the bishop of Salisbury, covered Sonning, Arborfield, Ruscombe, Sandhurst, and Wokingham, but even small manors could include two or more hamlets as well as places which later became individual parishes. Wexham and Hedgerley were part of Eton Manor in 1086, and the hamlet of Eton Wick may also have already come into existence. Related villages, such as Sulhamstead Bannister and Sulhamstead Abbots, are almost always given as one place. But serious as these difficulties may be, they do not detract from the overall pattern of settlement with its striking contrast between the densely populated northern area of scarps and vales and the more lightly settled southern and eastern regions.

35 *Collecting data for Domesday Book.*

Well-watered valleys, fertile soils and the proximity of downland pastures made northern Berkshire a prosperous area where dairy farming and cheese making were already well established. There were three lines of springline villages lying at the foot of the limestone, greensand and chalk escarpments. The chalk uplands were almost devoid of settlements, but there were plenty of villages and farmland in the valleys of the Lambourn, Kennet, Thames, and other smaller rivers of southern and central Berkshire. On the light acid soils and stiff clays of the south-east, however, the population and prosperity was markedly less, however it was measured—by the density of settlements or number of families, by the amount of meadow, or the number of plough teams. Surprisingly Domesday Book also records little woodland in south-eastern Berkshire, although this was the area of Windsor Forest. The number of pigs which should be paid annually as rent (pannage) is recorded for some of the adjacent manors, but the Forest was largely outside the scope of Domesday Book. Pannage figures indicate that the rest of southern Berkshire and the southern parishes of Buckinghamshire were also still quite wooded; Datchet, for example, owed pannage for 300 pigs. In contrast there was an almost complete absence of pannage figures for the downland and northern vales, though once again Domesday entries are deceptive, for Bagley and Commer Woods certainly existed at this date.

Only three, or maybe four, Berkshire settlements were large enough to be called towns in 1086—Wallingford with a population of between two and three thousand, Reading much smaller with some six or seven hundred inhabitants, and (Old) Windsor with almost five hundred. The fourth, unnamed in Domesday Book, was part of the Manor of Ulvritone, and had a population of around two hundred and fifty. Wallingford and Reading were designated boroughs, a term which should imply some kind of self-government in contrast to the rural manors which came under the jurisdiction of their lords. The Domesday Book word in this part of Britain for what has been interpreted as urban properties is *hagae*, and it is the 95 hagae in (Old) Windsor and 51 in Ulvritone (Newbury) that has led historians to suggest that these manors included towns and were not merely large rural manors.

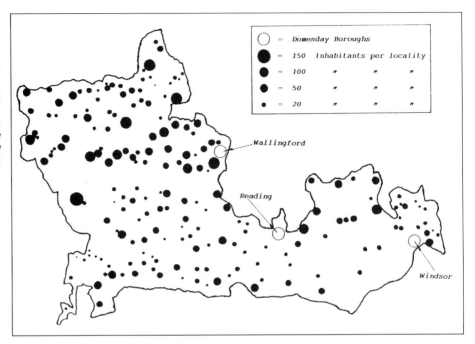

36 *Berkshire population according to the entries in Domesday Book of 1086; the number of people given probably represent families, rather than individuals. The contrast between the fertile, densely populated Vale of the White Horse and the sparsely populated area of Windsor Forest is clear.*

But how should one consider other places which had hagae, from Thatcham with 12 to Aldermaston with a mere seven? There is no easy answer, but it is safer to say that in 1086 Berkshire had four towns and several other places with some urban characteristics. Ulvritone is a name no longer in use, but its relatively large number of house plots and increased taxable value, rising from £9 to £24 between 1066 and 1086, suggests the foundation of the town we know as Newbury soon after the Conquest.

Surprisingly, Abingdon was not listed as a borough or a town, and there is no mention of an urban population, except for 10 merchants in the adjacent manor of Barton. Abingdon Abbey was the greatest landowner in the county after the King, holding more than thirty Berkshire manors and large tracts of land in Oxfordshire and elsewhere, but as yet there would appear to be no town serving the abbey. However, sometime during his reign, King William granted the monks the right to hold a market and collect the market tolls.

Thirteen other ecclesiastical institutions held estates in Berkshire, including Battle Abbey which held the lordship of part of Reading, and the Bishop of Salisbury who held three manors, including Sonning which spanned the county from the Thames to the Hampshire border. Forty-eight lay tenants-in-chief held land in the county, including some of William's closest and trusted followers, but for the most part their Berkshire holdings were few and their important residences were usually elsewhere in the country. For example, of William Peverel's 98 manors (mainly in Northamptonshire and Nottinghamshire, including Nottingham Castle), only one was in Berkshire.

V   *Ardington, near Wantage.*

VI   *Childrey village pond, near Wantage.*

VII *Long Bridge on the Thames just south of Eton Wick in the 1970s.*

VIII *Horse-drawn narrow boat on the Kennet and Avon Canal at Dun Mill, Hungerford.*

Three Norman barons had their main residence in Berkshire—Geoffrey de Mandeville, who established a house and priory at Hurley, Miles Crispin whose honour was centred on Wallingford Castle which came into his possession through his marriage to Robert D'Oyley's daughter, and Walter FitzOther, constable of Windsor Castle. Listed amongst the minor tenants were a few English men and women who retained their estates, but over the greater part of the county Berkshire peasants were under Norman rule. They were not slaves, but 'unfree', bound to their manors by obligation and work services.

Towns and Boroughs

Newbury, it is thought, was founded by the lord of Ulvritone, Ernulf De Hesdin, on part of the manor which lay south of the Kennet, along the north/south highway leading from Oxford and the Midlands to Southampton. By 1086 it had its own church which a few years later De Hesdin gave to the Abbey of Preaux in Rouen. Such gifts were a normal means by which lords gained the prayers of the monks, and the abbey gained the financial benefits of tithes and church offerings. De Hesdin, however, fell foul of William II and in 1096 found it expedient to leave the country on a pilgrimage to the Holy Land. His manors passed to other lords. In 1189 occurs the earliest known reference to burgesses, the name given to privileged householders in a town. Newbury already had a market and by 1204 a town bailiff. Sometime earlier St Bartholomew's Hospital had been built for the care of the sick and aged, and in 1215 King John granted the hospital the right to hold a two-day fair. The town was also concerned in this grant, for the townsfolk had the right to chose the master of the hospital. In 1275 Newbury was important enough to send two representatives to Parliament, and again in 1302 and 1337 when it was referred to as a 'borough'.

Exactly what is meant by the term 'borough' is uncertain; it was rarely used with legal exactness, but clearly Newbury had become separated from its parent manor and in some measure had begun to manage its own affairs. Abingdon, Reading, Wallingford and New Windsor also sent representatives to Parliament, but for these and other Berkshire towns, except Windsor and Wallingford, the struggle for independence lasted the whole of the Middle Ages.

Thatcham's urban beginnings are older than Newbury's, but its development into a town was much slower and intricately linked with the foundation of Reading Abbey by Henry I in 1121. Thatcham had been a royal manor, one of several which Henry gave to the abbey either as part of its initial endowment or soon after. The king also granted the abbey the right to hold a weekly market at Thatcham on Sundays, a privilege which brought financial benefits through the collection of market tolls and encouragement to traders and merchants and thus to the growth of prosperity. Most early medieval towns had little or no industry, and the markets and annual fairs were the centre of their commercial life.

37 *Newbury Borough seal.*

Despite royal and ecclesiastical encouragement, the market at Thatcham did not do well. Newbury was only three miles away and much better situated. The two towns, it would seem, had both been granted Sunday markets—a situation which hints at a story of deliberate rivalry. Indeed the townsfolk of Newbury objected so strongly to the new market at Thatcham that in 1160 they came in force, overturning stalls, damaging produce and causing a pitched battle in the main street. Reading Abbey sought royal protection, and Henry responded by issuing letters directing that the monks be allowed to hold their market there 'freely and fully' without interference. In 1218 it was felt expedient to change Thatcham's market day to Thursday.

The 13th century was a boom period for towns, and for a while Thatcham appears to have thrived. The right to hold an annual fair was granted in 1222, and by the end of the century the town had grown considerably, its built-up area spreading along the highway which linked London and Bristol. In 1304 a small chapel, which still survives, was built to serve the population at the eastern extremity of this ribbon development. Two years later Thatcham was taxed as a borough for the first time, and numerous surviving early 14th-century deeds record the sale of burgage plots. These were tenements which could be freely sold or rented in contrast to those in rural manors which were burdened by work services and other dues to the manorial lord. They were a characteristic feature of towns, and were occupied by the burgesses—the merchants, craftsmen and shopkeepers who made the settlement a town rather than a village. In many towns such men (and occasionally women) joined together to form merchant and craft guilds, and it was often through these guilds that the townsfolk sought to govern

38 *The medieval daughter chapel of St Thomas the Martyr was built in 1300 to serve the population at the eastern extremity of Thatcham.*

their own affairs. This might be achieved by buying or leasing privileges, or, if sufficiently powerful and rich, then the burgesses might be able to purchase a royal charter making the town a free, fully self-governing borough with its own council, chief officer (often called mayor) and borough courts. None of this appears to have happened in Thatcham. It remained subservient to Reading Abbey with no merchants' guild, but like Newbury the town became separated from the rural manor. In this case the original manor was divided, one part becoming known as the 'manor of the borough of Thatcham', the other as 'Thatcham alias Henwick' from the name of the country residence of the monks of Reading near Thatcham..

There was conflict over market rights in another Berkshire town—Abingdon—this time more persistently and with different results. The story begins in Henry I's reign when the King ordered an investigation into the rights and privileges of Abingdon Abbey. The abbot produced a charter and, when this was declared a forgery, he purchased a new one at a cost of 300 marks (£200) which confirmed the abbey's right to hold a market. This did not silence the opposition from the rival towns of Oxford and Wallingford, and in 1154 men from the two towns joined forces to attack the abbot's market. They brought with them a writ from Henry II which ordered a limitation to the range of produce which could be sold at Abingdon. Led by the constable of Wallingford Castle, the men marched into Abingdon and tried to clear the market place by force. The abbot's retainers, however, were too strong and foiled the attempt. Once again the Wallingford men took their case to the King, but, when enquiry had been made through the Berkshire county court and a court at Oxford, the abbot's

39 *Abingdon Abbey.*

rights were upheld. Further complaints to the king resulted in confirmation of the weekly market. Only in the matter of wares arriving by boat were any restrictions laid down.

There was clearly a town at Abingdon by this date, founded perhaps by the abbey itself. Later records show the existence of burgage plots, but all the rights to hold markets and fairs were in the hands of the bailiffs appointed by the abbot. They also held the fortnightly borough court, the twice yearly court leet, and a court of pie-powder which dealt with market disputes. The profits from all these were the rightful dues of the abbey. It was an arrangement which the members of the growing trading community resented, and by 1202 they had begun acting together as a body, most likely through a religious guild known as the fraternity of the Holy Cross which met at the church of St Helen's. In 1296 a number of townsmen attacked the abbot's bailiff, and in the early 14th century they stopped the fair taking place and took the proceeds of the market. In 1327 they were joined by the mayor and commonalty from Oxford and together they sacked the abbey and burnt down the market house. There were other attempts by the townsfolk to gain control of the market and to have a voice in the government of the town—but with little success for another hundred years. Such struggles and partial success were the fate of other towns in the country which were dominated by a great abbey, such as Reading, St Albans and Bury St Edmunds.

Reading had been named a royal borough in Domesday Book, but whatever independent status this conveyed was lost when the town was given to Reading Abbey as part of its foundation endowment. Here too there was

conflict between the townsfolk and the abbey officials who were accused of being oppressive and using unfair practices when carrying out their duties. Eventually in 1253 the abbot took the matter to the king's court and there the burgesses put forward their claim for the right of self-government. They lost, but the King granted the merchants a new charter giving them the right to buy and sell free of tolls in Reading or elsewhere in the county. Its guild merchant also came to a compromise agreement with the abbot whereby the abbey continued to preside over the town's court of justice and took rents for guild privileges, and in turn the guild gained the right to have a guildhall and other property and to organise their own trading affairs. Each year

40 *The Inner Gateway of Reading Abbey.*

the abbot chose one of their members to be their warden, a post which by the beginning of the 14th century was being styled 'mayor'.

By that date New Windsor was also a borough with its own burgesses and mayor. Its development, however, was not marred by rivalry although it grew at the expense of the Saxon town of (Old) Windsor. The earliest reference to the new town occurs in 1121, and historians believe that the town was deliberately laid out early in the 12th century, either on land belonging to the king's manor of (Old) Windsor, or possibly on that of Orton, a manor close to the castle hill held by Walter FitzOther, the constable of the castle. Tenants were encouraged to move to the new town from (Old) Windsor, and within a few decades Old Windsor had become a rural area. New Windsor was a very small town, and two centuries later, when numerous deeds make it possible to catch a glimpse of its streets and buildings, there were still only six main streets and one parish church. In contrast, by then Reading had three parish churches, and the walled town of Wallingford as many as eleven.

The market in Windsor lay opposite the castle gate with its ditch, bridge and barbican. Today the narrow cobbled streets follow the same line as the passageways between the medieval market stalls and tenements. Church Street was once called Fish Street and the butchers' shambles were located behind the present Guildhall. The town prospered and grew, spreading into the manors of Clewer and Windsor Underore which lay between the castle hill and the Thames. A bridge was built across the Thames sometime before 1236 when five oaks from Windsor Forest were provided for its upkeep. Windsor was also a small port, and there were wharves along the river front on either side of the bridge.

Until 1277 the town was under the jurisdiction of the constable of Windsor Castle; it was he who was responsible for collecting the king's taxes and dispensing justice in the manor courts held, no doubt, in the castle. By this date, however, the town had an active and flourishing merchants' guild able to bargain—and pay—for a borough charter from Edward I. It was a very important step, for by this charter the town burgesses became freemen, able to hold their own borough courts and manage their own financial affairs. Maintenance of the bridge was also their responsibility, although it lay outside the area of the borough, and soon after they received their charter the townsfolk petitioned for their right to collect tolls from all who travelled over or under the bridge. The charter also stated that the county gaol was to be at Windsor, and so it was for a few decades, until in 1314 a petition to the King complained that Windsor was too remote, and too small to provide sufficient food for the prisoners, 'whereby the prisoners die immediately, as well the innocent as the guilty'. Sometime later the gaol was removed to Reading which was rivalling Wallingford and more centrally situated in the county. Before the end of the 13th century Windsor had its own corporate seal, and by the mid-14th century the town had its own council and mayor which had evolved from the merchants' guild that had brought the borough into existence.

The 12th and 13th centuries were a period of rapid population growth, and at least a half-dozen or so other places in Berkshire showed signs of urban development. Aldermaston, Cookham, Hungerford, Faringdon, Lambourn, Wantage and Wargrave were styled as towns or boroughs in one or more medieval documents; all had a market. Wokingham also had a market, granted by the Bishop of Salisbury in 1219. The town was founded jointly by the Bishop and Dean of Salisbury to serve this rather remote part of the county, though it remained under the jurisdiction of the lord of the manor of Sonning (the Bishop) throughout the medieval period. The Bishop took quit rents from about two thirds of the properties in the town, and the Dean took the rest.

The origins of Maidenhead were rather different from those of any of the other Berkshire towns. There is no mention of burgesses or burgage tenure in any of the surviving medieval records, and all through the Middle Ages the settlement remained under the jurisdiction of the two manors in which it lay—Bray and Cookham. The boundary between the two lay along the High Street, and it would seem likely that the town was laid out by the lords of the two manors sometime after the development of the highway as the main long distance route westwards out of London. Historians have argued that in the late Saxon period the crossing of the Thames was at Cookham, where there had been a Saxon burh and a monastery, and where in 1086 there was a new market. By 1297, however, the important bridge was at Maidenhead. It is mentioned for the first time in the Patent Rolls of that year because the bridge was in need of repair, but both bridge and town may have been built a hundred or more years earlier. What is certain is that the bridge lay at the junction of the two manors and that Maidenhead had developed from a Saxon village known as South Ellington more than half a mile to the west of the bridge. The second part of its new name means 'wharf', but whether the wharf was next to the Thames or alongside the bridge within the town may never be known.

If the little town was deliberately founded, it would appear to have received few privileges. Nevertheless a rudimentary form of independent government did develop. A chapel was built by the residents about 1270, carefully positioned to straddle the parish boundary. No permission for this chapel had been obtained from the churches of Bray and Cookham, and the bishop issued an interdict forbidding its use and threatening excommunication on any clergy who dared to hold services there. For half a century it stood unused, until the ban was lifted and the chapel officially opened in 1324. In 1337 Edward III made a grant to the bailiffs and good men of 'Maidenhithe' of the right to collect pontage (bridge tolls) from all who travelled over or under the bridge; earlier grants had been made to men appointed by the king. A guild was formed in 1451 with the dual purpose of maintaining a chantry, which had been founded a century earlier in the Maidenhead chapel, and taking responsibility for the upkeep of the bridge across the Thames.

Trade and Communications

Many Berkshire towns were sited at river crossings and, as in the case of Wallingford and Maidenhead, the crossings were crucial to their very foundation. But river travel was also important to their trade and there were wharves at Windsor, Maidenhead, Wallingford and Reading where recent excavations have revealed the complexity of the waterfront belonging to the town and abbey along the Kennet.

Our knowledge of the network of navigable rivers and roads which linked every village and town in Saxon and Norman Berkshire, however, is meagre. The Icknield Way which crosses the northern part of the county was one of four roads given the king's royal protection in the tenth century, and Saxon charters of north Berkshire parishes mention the Ridgeway and the Port Way which linked Wantage with the port or market of Wallingford. Domesday Book gives little information about either roads or river navigation except in the form of lists of obligations of royal tenants in Wallingford. They were required to serve the king by water as far upstream as Sutton Courtenay and downstream to Reading. They were also expected to provide horse transport to Blewbury and to Benson just across the Thames in Oxfordshire. The chronicle of Abingdon Abbey also refers to a road to London passing through Colnbrook in 1106 in connection with a gift of an *hospitium* to the abbey from Miles Crispin of Wallingford. Whether this was an inn or a religious guest house is now impossible to say, but for travellers it was a welcome place to stop before crossing the marshy valley of the Colne. There are other references to roads in contemporary documents, but it is not until the 14th century that we can begin to map the pattern of main roads crossing the county.

Around 1360 the oldest known official map of Britain was drawn by an unknown mapmaker; today it is known as Gough's Map after a former owner. It shows roads radiating out from London—but the pattern is not quite the same as it had been in Roman times, especially in Berkshire. The road to Calleva and Aqua Sulis (Bath) did not come back into use. The bridge at Staines (Roman *Pontes*) was not rebuilt until the 14th century, and long before this another westward highway had come into existence which crossed the Thames until Maidenhead. This was the Bristol Road (later known as the Bath Road), the forerunner of the A4, and it is depicted as passing through Colnbrook, Maidenhead, Reading, Newbury and Hungerford. Colnbrook and Maidenhead were important because of their

41 *Medieval wharf at Reading.*

42 *The market towns of medieval Berkshire and the roads shown on Gough's map of c.1360.*

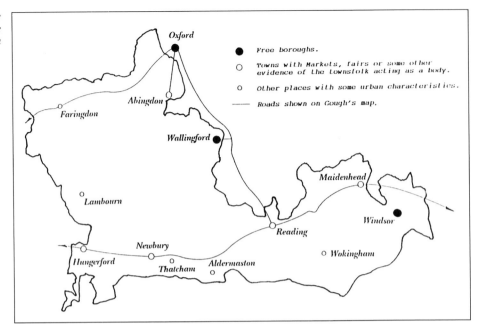

bridges and almost certainly came into existence because of the highway. Reading probably pre-dated the road, but during the 12th century its plan was radically altered as its economic focus moved from the market place outside St Mary's Church to the new market place outside the gate of the abbey. The markets and main streets of Newbury and Hungerford were located well south of the road; indeed strictly speaking the towns did not reach as far north as the Bristol Road, but the distinct southward curve of the road (before the 20th-century alterations obscured the pattern) suggests that a re-routing took place to bring travellers and traders into the towns. There is a similar curve on the road at Thatcham, no doubt brought about for the same reason.

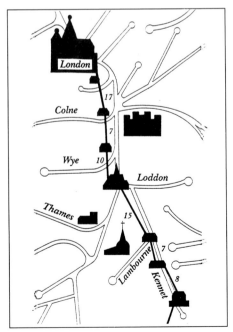

43 *Part of Gough's map depicted in outline. The road leads to Bristol; the mileages given are not correct by today's reckoning. The towns and villages shown are Brentford, Colnbrook, Maidenhead, Reading, Newbury, Hungerford, Marlborough, Wallingford and Abingdon.*

No other road out of London is shown passing through Berkshire. The forerunner of the A40 passes through Oxford, not Wallingford, though a branch line is shown connecting the two towns, and another leads through Faringdon to St David's in Wales. No road is shown linking Abingdon although a bird's-eye view of the abbey marks the town. This could be an example of the mapmaker's failure to complete that part of the map, but in 1360 Abingdon had no bridge across the Thames; road travellers had to cross at Wallingford or Oxford.

In 1416 Abingdon's Guild of the Holy Cross obtained a licence from the King to build a bridge, or rather two bridges linked by a causeway. Surprisingly the abbot does not seem to have supported the townsfolk and the land had first to be bought from the abbey. The bridges were paid for by donations and by money raised by the guild, and, when the guild received a charter of incorporation some 25 years later, its most important responsibility was the maintenance of the bridges. A considerable income might have been made from collecting tolls, but from the outset the bridges were free, an incentive to attract trade to the town. It was the final straw for the declining fortunes of Wallingford. The town, once the largest and most important in Berkshire, was now in a sorry state. There were many empty areas within the town walls and, out

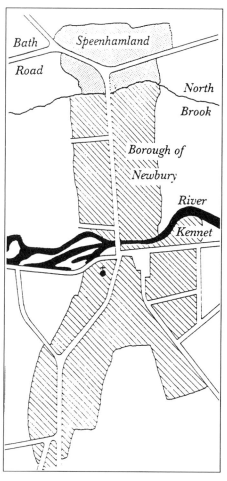

44 *Plan of the medieval town of Newbury showing the importance of the north/south route and the curve of the Bath Road towards the town. Note the northern boundary of the borough ran along the North Brook.*

of the 11 parish churches, only three were still in use. An inquisition taken in 1438 found that there were no more than 44 householders in the town— less than a tenth of the number listed in Domesday Book. Windsor was also suffering from a period of decline, but Reading in contrast now ranked as the largest town in the county and amongst the first 30 in the country according to wealth as measured by the taxes paid in 1334. By the 1520s tax records suggest that it had become the tenth richest provincial town in England.

Most medieval towns had a broad range of craftsmen and traders, such as brewers, butchers, carpenters, leather workers, mercers, smiths and victuallers, all mainly serving the town itself and its immediate hinterland through its weekly market. The woollen and cloth industry was rather different. In the early Middle Ages, wool was the country's most important export, and the Continental textile industry relied heavily on a supply of fine wool from England. Fine cloth was mostly imported, though the presence of fulling mills on many estates, including Elcot, a royal manor near Newbury,

45 *A king's messenger from a document in the Public Record Office.*

and weavers and dyers in towns are evidence for the manufacture of home-produced coarser clothes. By the mid-14th century the industry had changed. Cloth replaced wool as the country's major export, and the cloth-making industry began moving out of the towns into the countryside, probably to escape the restrictions of the town guilds. Many new mills were built on fast-running streams; in Berkshire these were mainly along the Kennet. Reading and Newbury flourished as market centres for the sale of wool and cloth; the division of the river into many streams gave Reading the advantage of a plentiful supply of water for washing and dyeing. Pack horse trains took their valuable loads of fine cloth along the Bristol Road to the great markets at Bristol and London from whence they were exported. Both Reading and Newbury were also sited on important north/south roads, though only one of them was shown on the Gough Map, giving the towns access to the Midlands and the south coast ports.

Fields and Forests

Everywhere in Berkshire there were villages and hamlets, most of which were much older than the manors or parishes in which they lay. The area of an 'ideal' parish might coincide with that of the manor and encompass a nucleated village, two or three large common fields, meadow and a village green, and woodland, but in reality there was almost unlimited diversity. Clewer parish had two villages, one centred on the church, manor house and mill, the other on a village green and a newer manor house belonging to the subsidiary manor of Clewer Brocas. There were probably two demesne farms, but only one system of common fields. There were two manors in Dedworth, a village around a green, but no church. In contrast Upton cum Chalvey had two separate field systems, each with three or more fields, common meadow and pasture, and Upton had a detached area of woodland. The hamlet of Slough which came into existence in the 12th century at a cross-roads on the Bristol road lay on the edge of both manors and spread into the neighbouring parish of Stoke Poges.

Perhaps the most striking visual feature of the medieval landscape was the common fields. It is thought that they came into being in the middle or late Saxon period in response to an expansion of population and the need for more arable land. Common fields are mentioned in 10th- and 11th-century documents relating to Ardington, Curridge, Harwell and Kingston Bagpuize. These fields were divided into a large number of strips and, although these were owned by individuals, after the harvest all those who had common rights could pasture their livestock on the grass growing through the stubble. The number of fields varied considerably. Great Coxwell had three fields, of which two fields were sown each year with wheat, oats, barley, rye and beans. Little Faringdon, Harwell and Woolstone had only two, while Eton had four—South Field, North Field, West Field and the Hyde; the first two have survived the centuries and were registered under the Commons Registration Act of 1965. With each man's land intermingled

with others, farming had to be a communal concern, organised by the village reeve under the jurisdiction of the manor court.

The 12th and 13th centuries were a period of expansion, and numerous records hint at the clearing of woodland for cultivation. The Pipe Roll of 1130 records large fines paid for assarts, small enclosed fields taken out of the waste or woodland. So much land was taken from Windsor Forest that disputes arose over the ownership of the tithes. One assart, aptly named Deulecress (may God increase it) was a bone of contention between Waltham Abbey in Essex, which held the church of New Windsor, and the Dean of Salisbury who claimed the tithes for Clewer. Eventually 12 honest knights were ordered to determine the parish boundary. By far the greater part of the report of a survey of Windsor Forest taken in 1333 is taken up with the details of enclosures 'contrary to the assize'. Many were no more than a cottage and garden, and neither they, nor larger enclosed fields, were considered any great offence, though in future the occupiers had to pay rent if on royal land, and no fence or ditch must impede the movement of the king's deer.

Windsor Forest land did not all belong to the king, nor was it one huge forest; it included individual woods with names like Brocwold and Easthurst, heathland and marshy areas, as well as farmland, towns and villages. Forest was a legal term for land subject to forest law, and in the early 13th century the whole of the county was within either Windsor Forest or Berkshire Forest until the latter was disafforested in 1225.

Forests and forest law protected the king's deer and the trees and undergrowth so necessary to their well-being, but more protective still were the parks with their fences, hedges and embankments designed to keep the game within. The most important was Windsor Great Park, which by several stages of enclosure reached its greatest extent in 1365. But there were many others in Berkshire, such as East Hampstead, Foxley and Foliejohn. Not all were within the Forest, or were owned by the king; Cippenham Park was created by Prince Richard, King John's younger son, around 1230.

Nationally the growth of population reached a peak in the early years of the 14th century and pressure on the land was at its greatest. New land was taken into cultivation, but frequent poor harvests and recurrent plagues

47 Medieval home-stead moat at Cippen-ham, Slough, where Richard Earl of Corn-wall had a manor house and deer park during the early 13th century.

brought a halt to the process, and the Black Death of 1349 brought a decline in the population from which the country did not recover for several generations. A few years earlier an enquiry concerning taxes brought complaints of failed harvests and sheep diseases in several Thames Valley parishes, including Tilehurst, Basildon and Streatley. Between 1313 and 1317 the number of sheep on the chalkland pastures of Inkpen declined from 468 to a mere 137. Marginal land was abandoned and some villages, like Seacourt in the parish of Wytham, were deserted. The customary tenants at Crookham were said to be 'all dead by the pestilence and their lands in the hands of the lord because there [was] no one who wants to buy or hire them'. Altogether over forty deserted villages have been identified in Berkshire, though not all belonged to this period.

The effects of the Black Death on Berkshire villages were severe rather than long lasting, and manors like Woolstone soon returned to pre-plague prosperity. The death of so many peasants, however, encouraged some manorial tenants to demand an end to feudal services and the payment of wages and rents instead of work service. On the manor of Bray conditions did change, but there are few signs of manorial lords in Berkshire freeing their tenants completely. Where manorial records survive, such as Brightwalton, North Moreton, and Frilsham, villeinage continued much as it had done since the 12th or 13th centuries. On the royal estates at Windsor and Eton work services were commuted to money in 1369, but here the cause was not the loss of labourers through death but Edward III's pressing need for money for his rebuilding programme at Windsor Castle. Only at Abingdon and Langley Marish (now part of Slough) is it known that there was active participation in the Peasants' Revolt of 1381.

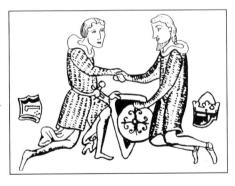

48 Richard, Earl of Cornwall, shaking hands with Nasir, a Saracen with whom Richard had made a treaty during the Crusade of 1241.

The all pervading church

It is difficult for residents of present-day Berkshire to comprehend the extent of the church's influence on the lives of the people of medieval Berkshire or the number of religious buildings. Every parish by now had its church, and several of the large parishes with a number of villages also had dependent chapels. Langley Marish was a chapelry of Wraysbury, and in the parish of Sonning there were chapels at Arborfield, Earley, Hurst, Ruscombe, Sandhurst, Sindlesham and Wokingham. These chapels were often parish churches in all but name, but they were not allowed in most cases to retain fees, offerings or tithes. By 1291, a third of the 189 Berkshire parish churches had been granted to monasteries or cathedrals. Most of them were now being served by vicars who were supplied by the religious houses and were only entitled to the small tithes; the great tithes from hay, corn and livestock were taken by the monastery. Large tithe barns, such as those at Great Coxwell and Cholsey, were built to hold the produce.

49 *John Henle, parish priest of Longworth, taken from a drawing in the Bodleian Library.*

Berkshire only had two great abbeys, those of Abingdon and Reading; but as holders of estates and churches the abbeys had control over the inhabitants of numerous Berkshire villages. As dispensers of hospitality, they entertained people of every class—kings, barons, merchants, poor travellers, pilgrims and lepers. Soon after its foundation, William of Malmesbury praised the 'unwearied and delightful hospitality' of Reading Abbey, and before the end of the century its monks had recorded more than thirty miracles performed there through the hand of St James, a gift to the abbey from its founder, Henry I. At Hurley there was a Benedictine priory, dependent on Westminster Abbey, and another at Wallingford which belonged to St Alban's Abbey. The Augustine Order of monks had priories at Bisham, Poughley and Sandleford; there was a nunnery at Bromhall near Sunningwell in Windsor Forest, and one at Ankerwick near Wraysbury. At Greenham and Bisham, the Knights Hospitallers had houses, though the latter became an Augustinian abbey in 1337.

The wave of religious enthusiasm which had encouraged the building of churches and monasteries changed direction in the 13th century with the introduction of friars into this country. They took religion into the market places and village streets. Unlike most monks and parish priests, they were trained to preach, and the visit of a grey friar from Reading or a Crutched

50 *Tithe barn at Great Coxwell, the largest in Berkshire.*

51   *A friar.*

friar from Donnington brought news and excitement into humdrum lives as well as a message from God.

The people of the Middle Ages had an essentially practical attitude to religion, one by which gifts of alms and endowments enabled the donor to quicken his passage to heaven through the cleansing fires of purgatory. Pilgrims travelled to shrines such as in Reading Abbey, the hermitage at St Leonard's deep in the forest near Clewer, and St Mary's Chapel at Caversham. Hospitals were founded for the poor and infirm. Berkshire had a wealth of such almshouses: three in Abingdon and others at Childrey, Fyfield, Hungerford, Lambourn, Newbury, Reading and Wallingford. Lepers and people with other disfiguring diseases could find a place to rest and be cared for at Hungerford, Reading, Windsor, Newbury and Wallingford, and in Caversham the ill could seek healing from the waters of St Anne's well, the chapel of which also served as toll house for the bridge. Maidenhead bridge also had a chapel and a hermit to collect the tolls.

Rich men also founded chantries, chapels within a church where a priest said mass daily for the souls of the founder and his family. At Clewer, the chapel is still known by the name of its founder, Sir John Brocas. At Shottesbrook and Wallingford, communities of priests known as colleges likewise prayed for the souls of their founders, but perhaps the most splendid examples of such colleges were those at Eton where Henry VI founded a school, college and almshouse in 1440, and Windsor where the first St George's Chapel was built by Edward III. It was, according to his own words, built as a bargain with God. A century later Edward IV began the work of rebuilding the chapel. It is the most ambitious 15th-century building in Berkshire—and one of the last of that kind of church to be built in England.

52   *Eton College was founded by Henry VI in 1440. The church is the oldest part of the college, but is far smaller than the founder's original plan.*

4
Reformation, Revolution and Restoration 1486-1714

In 1485 the Battle of Bosworth heralded the beginning of a new era and a welcome period of peace after decades of sporadic fighting. There was a new royal family on the English throne—the Tudors—but the England of Henry VII was a far cry from that of Henry VIII or Elizabeth I. Compared with the Continent, it was a backward country suffering from a long period of population decline. The towns were small and their decayed buildings an outward sign of difficult times. Earlier in the 15th century Windsor had appealed to the King for a reduction in taxes because its houses were in ruins, its people 'moneyless'; the petition exaggerated, but taxes were reduced from £17 to £10, and when prosperity came back to the town most of its medieval houses were pulled down. In contrast, by the end of the Stuart era in the early 18th century, England was one of the wealthiest nations in the world. But in the intervening two and a half centuries under

53 *Handing over money.*

54 *Ockenden, a 15th-century manor.*

the Tudors and Stuarts the country had passed through religious and agricultural upheavals, a great rebuilding of town and country, periods of recession and prosperity, another civil war, and a revolution in the government of both country and county.

The Rural County

Tudor Berkshire had no sharp division between town and country such as we see today, for the trades and markets in the town depended on the produce from the farms, and most towns still contained fields and commons within their boundaries. Reading was the largest town, with a population of around three thousand, which was not much greater than Wallingford had been at the end of the 11th century. Tax assessments suggest that the population of few parishes exceeded a hundred families, and most had considerably less. On a large number of estates the old ways of farming persisted; open fields and commons were found in every part of the county, and here and there, as in Stratfield Mortimer and Coleshill, unfree villeins still performed work services for the lords of the manor. Almost every inhabitant in rural parishes had an interest in the land; renting even an acre or two could make the difference between poverty and relative economic security. For the gentry and nobility, wealth still lay with their landed estates.

Corn was grown in all parts of Berkshire, and from the beginning of Elizabeth's reign considerable amounts were sent down river to London. The trade grew in size and importance, so much so that when movement of grain was stopped during the Civil War, the inhabitants of Reading claimed with some truth that it lost the town at least £2,000 'in ready money' each week. Most farms, however, had a mixed economy, and large numbers of sheep were kept on the sweet pasture of the downlands where the thin chalk soils were made productive by dung from the sheep. Wool and cloth accounted for more than three-quarters of England's export trade, and in this Berkshire played a vital part. Berkshire wool was of a high quality suitable for making fine broadcloths and kerseys, the name given to narrow cloth. In 1574 it ranked as one of the four highest priced wools in England. Marketing the wool was in the hands of wool merchants who mainly lived in the country districts where they made their purchases; thus for example, Richard and John Yates of Charney Basset and Longworth were members of the English Company of Merchants of the Staple through which the export trade was organised. In 1620 Francis Moore, lord of the manor of East Ilsley, obtained a charter to hold a monthly corn and sheep market which attracted buyers from many parts of southern England.

The main centres of the cloth trade were Reading, Abingdon and Newbury. In the early 16th century Newbury's chief clothier, John Winchcombe (nicknamed Jack of Newbury), had an international reputation. He was an entrepreneur, and his business was concerned with all stages of the industry from buying the raw wool to selling the finished cloth in the

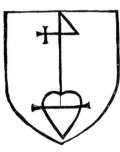

55 *The Yates' merchant mark, taken from a drawing in the Bodleian Library.*

great London market. In Elizabeth's reign Thomas Deloney wrote a romantic story of his life, historical fiction rather than a biography, but according to this he employed more than six hundred men, women and children, as well as wainsmen and carts to carry the cloth to London. No doubt this was an exaggeration, but Jack did make a fortune, and his cloth was so highly prized that his name lived on as a standard for high quality. In 1549, thirty years after his death, a thousand 'Winchcombe kerseys' were sent to the English envoy in Antwerp. It was mainly through his generosity that the church of St Nicholas in Newbury was rebuilt between 1509 and 1533.

56 *Richard and John Yates of Charney Basset, from a drawing in the Bodleian Library.*

57 *East Ilsley Fair, c.1918. For almost three hundred years this was one of the most important sheep fairs in southern England.*

Newbury's other famous clothier was Thomas Dolman who, in 1581, built for himself Shaw House, (now a school) a beautiful mansion costing £10,000, after he retired from trade. By this date the industry was depressed, partly through over-production, and there was wide-scale unemployment. Although cloth manufacture continued in west and north Berkshire, the golden era of England's woollen textile industry was over. The resentment felt by Dolman's former workers is summed up in a rhyme written at the time:

Lord, have mercy upon us, miserable sinners
Thomas Dolman has built a new house, and turned away all his spinners.

Reading also had its wealthy clothiers, three of whom had sons (William Laud, John Kendrick and Sir Thomas White) who left the town to make their fortunes elsewhere. The most famous of these was William Laud who became Archbishop of Canterbury in 1633. Both Reading and Windsor benefited from the money he left, but it was his contemporary, John Kendrick who was so important to the twists of fortune which beset the clothing industry. Kendrick died in 1625 leaving a bequest of £7,000 to Reading Corporation and £4,000 to Newbury, on condition that the mayor and burgesses in both towns provided a house, 'fit and commodious for setting of the poor on work therein, with a fair garden adjoining'. Such workhouses where the poor could be provided with materials for spinning and weaving are found in other towns, such as Windsor. But what seemed good in theory was not always so in practice, since the poor did not always produce quality workmanship, and the goods could undercut those of the other manufacturers. In Reading the money was mismanaged, and much of the surplus money which should have been used to help poor cloth manufacturers was appropriated by the members of the Corporation or their

58 *John Kendrick, son of a successful Reading clothier, who left bequests to the clothing towns of Reading and Newbury.*

friends, whose businesses flourished at the expense of the rest. Instead of promoting the trade, Kendrick's bequest was a major factor in hastening its decline. At Newbury the money was used to build the fine building (the surviving wing, known as Cloth Hall, is now a museum) where 60 people, plus 14 apprentices, were employed making cloth. Cloth production was also strong in the surrounding villages; the inhabitants of Shaw, Speen, Thatcham and Greenham were employed in the production of yarn, and several villages had their own fulling mills. But, although the cloth trade struggled on, the days of prosperity had gone, leaving cloth workers amongst the distressed and unemployed.

The high profits enjoyed by the wool industry in the early Tudor period had encouraged landowners and farmers to enclose areas of pasture. In some cases arable land was also converted to pasture, which meant fewer farm workers and the evictions of tenants whose land had been taken. In the most extreme cases whole parishes were cleared of cottages, as for example Eaton Hastings in the north west of the county, and Tulwick near Wantage, where one John Saunders enclosed 55 acres in 1500 and evicted the last four tenants from the village. Worried about depopulation in many parts of the country, the government ordered a number of enquiries. In 1517 the commissioners reported that in Berkshire land had been enclosed for sheep pasture in 25 parishes, including Barkham, Milton, Southcot, and Woolley where a hundred acres were taken out of cultivation. At Milton 18 people lost employment and the two plough teams were put out of use. Arable farming, however, was also profitable, and among those farmers who did well were the Loders of Harwell who in four generations rose from humble husbandmen to gentlemen. For ten years, 1610 -1620, Robert Loder kept meticulous accounts. He farmed more than three hundred acres on which he grew wheat, barley, pulses and vetches. There were also extensive orchards, and on the downs he had a 65-acre enclosure for his sheep.

Enclosure for pasture was not the only way that landowners were maximising their profits from farming. Engrossing is the term used for combining two or more farms and, whether it was to improve livestock or arable farming, it usually meant the loss of a farmhouse and the eviction of the occupiers. At Fulscot, according to the enquiry, 29 people were turned out after three farms had been engrossed and three houses were pulled down. There were many more cases than those listed in the government enquiry. At Upton in Slough, members of the Urlwyn family leased the manor house and demesne farm during the mid-16th century and, though few records survive to tell us details of their activities, they acquired almost all the land in two of Upton's open fields. They also obtained ownership of most of South Field belonging to the adjacent manor of Chalvey, to the detriment of its inhabitants. Land was also taken from fields and commons by landowners rich enough to create or enlarge parks. A hundred acres were enclosed at Hampstead Marshall for this purpose, 60 acres at Hurst, and smaller amounts in several other places. On the whole, however, Berkshire did not suffer badly in this direction, and at least one park was turned into farmland. This was Cippenham Park which became Cippenham Court Farm in the 15th century, sometime after it came into the hands of the Molyns family of Stoke Poges. The outline of the park pale can still be traced in hedgerows first planted some five hundred years ago.

Religious Change

The seeds of religious change had been sown long before the Tudor period. In the late 14th century John Wycliffe had questioned almost every aspect of Church beliefs and advocated the translation of the Bible into English.

He was the first of the religious critics known as Lollards. In 1412 a Wokingham man was prosecuted for Lollardy and by the 1420s there was a 'glorious and sweet society of faithful followers' in the Vale of the White Horse with members from Abingdon, Buscot, Faringdon, East Ginge, Hanney, Steventon and Wantage. In 1431, under the leadership of one William Perkins, they marched from East Hendred to Abingdon where they attacked the abbey. As in other cases the rising failed and Perkins was executed. It was the last of the Lollard rebellions, but there was a small rising in Wokingham in 1434, and in 1490 Thomas Taylor, a fuller at Newbury, was charged with possessing Lollard books and denying the doctrine of transubstantiation. At Letcombe Basset the priest John Whithorn attracted a group of believers who were charged in 1499 with possessing copies of the gospel and other books in English. In 1518 Christopher Shoemaker of Newbury was burnt to death for reading the Bible out loud in English.

To the Church, the Lollards were heretics who must be punished and prevented from spreading their beliefs. England's break away from Rome and Henry VIII's assumption of the position of the Supreme Head of the English Church in 1534, however, had little to do with religious reform, and rather more with Henry's desire to marry Anne Boleyn and sire a male heir. There may have been need to reform the monastic houses, but Henry's decision to dissolve them was more concerned with replenishing the royal coffers. The operation took place in two stages. First the smaller houses worth less than £200 were closed in 1536; there were nine of these in Berkshire and one more in Wraysbury which is now within the county. (Bromhall Nunnery at Sunninghill had been closed in 1521.)

Berkshire religious houses on the eve of dissolution

	Houses	Annual income
Dissolved in 1538	Reading Abbey	£1,908 14s 0d
	Abingdon Abbey	£1,876 10s 9d
Dissolved in 1536	Bisham	£ 185 11s 0d
	Hurley Priory	£ 121 18s 5d
	Poughley Priory	£ 71 11s 7d
	Greenham	£ 36 2s 5d
	Donnington Priory	£ 28 0s 0d
	Sandleford	£ 18 0s 0d
	Ankerwyk	not known
	Reading Priory	not known
	Wallingford Priory	not known

An investigation by Thomas Cromwell's commissioners revealed few scandals, though plenty of examples of lax monasteries and nunneries. Two years later the great abbeys were closed. One of the earliest was Abingdon where the abbot and monks accepted the decision—and generous pensions— with little protest. Reading Abbey, however, held out to the last, the abbot, Hugh Faringdon, refusing to surrender the abbey, its treasures or its revenues.

Hugh had been on good terms with Henry VIII. He had signed the petition to the Pope urging him to hasten the proceedings for annulment and had offered the abbey's library facilities for Henry's lawyers, but none of this stood him in good stead. He and two of his monks were judged and condemned as common criminals, and were hanged, drawn and quartered; their mutilated bodies hung in a gibbet near the abbey gate, a dire warning of Henry's might and the cruelty of kings.

By 1540 all the monasteries had gone, ransacked of their ornaments, plate, relics, and money. During the remainder of Henry VIII's reign, the

59 *Ruins of Reading Abbey. Most of the usable material was stripped off the building in the 16th century.*

site of Reading Abbey remained Crown property, and little further despoliation took place until 1548 when, at the instigation of Edward Seymour, Protector of the Realm, the lead from the roofs was stripped. Stone was taken for road mending and other buildings as far away as Windsor. Most other Berkshire religious houses suffered a similar fate, and today all that can be seen are ruins. Greyfriars Priory at Reading, on the other hand, was not destroyed. Henry gave this to the town for use as a town hall, as the hall in use was alleged to be much too small and disturbed by the noise of the washerwomen using the River Kennet close by.

Although the abbey and priory buildings and lands were at first taken into the hands of the Crown, most were soon given or sold to members of the Court, county families, wealthy merchants, or town corporations. The site of Abingdon Abbey was bought by Sir Thomas Seymour, but its vast estates were purchased by a variety of people, amongst them Richard Warde, keeper of the royal treasury, who bought the manor of Winkfield. From the Reading Abbey estate John Winchcombe, the wealthy clothier from Newbury, bought the manors of Thatcham and Bucklebury; he demolished the old manor house at Bucklebury and built in its place a fine Tudor mansion. Windsor Corporation acquired the manor of Windsor Underore which had been given to Reading Abbey by Queen Matilda, and at Bisham the former priory was turned into a house, the home of the Hoby family.

The Dissolution brought about the greatest change of land ownership since the Norman Conquest, but the changes went much deeper than the loss of buildings and the redistribution of land holdings. Parish churches held by abbeys and convents now had new patrons, and the tithes had to be paid to lay owners. It also meant the loss of a whole range of services which the religious houses had performed. Gone were most of the travellers' guests houses, the leper houses, hermitages and hospitals. The Dissolution was also responsible for adding to the number of homeless and unemployed—not the monks and nuns who were given pensions—but the many lay servants. Few dared to oppose the King, but in 1542 James Mallet, a canon of St George's Chapel, Windsor, was burnt to death for speaking out against the Dissolution.

In 1538 Henry VIII's policies took religious change into every parish with his injunction that each church should have a Bible written in English, though labourers and all women, except gentlewomen, were forbidden to read it. Parishes were also ordered to keep registers of baptisms, marriages and burials. The records of a number of Berkshire parishes show that he was promptly obeyed. The parish registers of Barkham, Basildon, Binfield, Bucklebury and many others all begin in 1538 or the following year. Church services, however, had not changed; instead the old beliefs had become compulsory, and to deny any of the points laid down in the Six Article Statute of 1540 became a crime punishable by death. In 1543 three Windsor men—Henry Filmer, Anthony Pierson and Robert Testwood—became Berkshire's first martyrs under this law. They were burnt at the stake on the low ground to the north of the castle, an event which was all the more terrible because the men who accused them of heresy were later arrested and found guilty of perjury.

60 *In 1548 three men accused of being heretics were burnt at the stake at Windsor.*

The pressing need for money was again the cause of destructive changes under Edward VI which began with the suppression of chantries and guilds.

The reports of the commissioners are often the only source of information on these chantries, and the picture revealed is a very mixed one. Some, like those of the Brocas Chantry of Clewer, no longer had a priest, others, like the Englefield Chantry at Reading and the John Leigh chantry at Binfield, were alleged to have been dissolved without licence and the income pocketed by the local patrons. In other cases the chantry priest played an important role in parish life, responsible for an almshouse or a school. There were seven such almshouses and five schools with chantry priests acting as school-masters in Berkshire. Several of the almshouses and schools survived; the Childrey almshouses and those founded by John Estbury at Lambourn are still in use today although not in the original buildings. The Holy Trinity guild at Windsor had paid a priest to run a small grammar school, but there was no schoolmaster when the royal commissioners made their survey, and Windsor did not get another grammar school until this century. There is little evidence that people protested against the loss of the chantries and guilds, though no doubt most would have been too frightened of the con-sequences of any rebellion. A few churchwardens pre-empted the removal of church goods by the commissioners and themselves sold the valuables; the churchwardens of St Lawrence, Reading received £47 18s. 0d. for their church plate and used most of the money for street paving.

Whereas Henry VIII's religion might be described as Roman Catholic without the Pope, that of Edward VI was fervently Protestant. Church ser-vices were ordered to be held in English, not Latin; Boxford churchwardens' accounts record the purchase of the new English prayer book in 1549, the year it was first published. In 1551 parish churches in Berkshire were once again surveyed: with what fear and apprehension did the clergymen and churchwardens meet the commissioners? The veneration of saints and the use of anything Roman Catholic was now forbidden; monuments were de-faced and wall paintings covered with white paint. In 1553 Thomas Vachell of Coley, the commissioner responsible for Berkshire, began the task of stripping the county's churches of their valuables. The pillage continued for eight months under his direction, and nearly 1,500 ounces of silver and gold plate were sent to London from Berkshire. The parish church now had a very different appearance—but in all too short a time it was to change once again when Queen Mary brought back Roman Catholicism.

During Mary's reign (1553-1558) parishioners were required at their own expense to re-equip their churches for Catholic services, and strong Protestant priests, like John Leke of Purley who had married, were deprived of their livings. Ancient heresy laws were revived, and during the five years of Mary's reign more than 300 people were burnt at the stake for their faith, including three at Newbury, a town which recent research has shown to have been strongly and obstinately Protestant. During the early 17th century it 'possessed a national reputation for religious zeal, unshared with any other town in the county'.

Queen Elizabeth brought back Protestantism. In 1559, one year after she took the throne, Parliament passed the Act of Supremacy which made her the supreme head of the Church of England, and an Act of Uniformity which made attendance at church compulsory. Clergymen and others holding public offices were required to take the oath, and those who could not, like the Rev Richard Gatskill of Purley, lost their living. The colourful story of the Vicar of Bray who was said to have remained parish priest at Bray through four religious changes cannot be substantiated by evidence. There were at least two vicars at Bray during this period (and maybe four)—Simon Simonds, a conservative Papist, and Simon Aleyn, a fanatical Protestant reformer.

Once again parishes were put to the expense of altering their churches. At Wantage the rejected altar stone was hidden under the church steps where it was found in the 19th century. Some priests continued to celebrate Mass in secret and, when in the 1570s Catholic priests were smuggled into the country, they were supported by several Berkshire families, such as the Hindesleys of Beenham and East Ilsley, the Morris family of Great Coxwell, and the Perkins of Brimpton. Father William Hopkins lived with the Yates family of Buckland, hiding when necessary in a priest hole in the manor house. The newly built Ufton Court, which became the home of William Perkins, had six priest holes and became one of a chain of safe houses for missionary priests travelling inland from the coast.

Roman Catholics who did not attend church were known as recusants and fined at the Quarter Sessions. Ordinary villagers and townsfolk usually paid only 1s. each quarter, but members of the gentry, such as Thomas Vachell, could be fined as much as £50 per year. In 1586 the fines from 53 Berkshire recusants mounted to £138 6s. 6d. Despite persistent anti-Catholic legislation, some Berkshire families remained true to their faith, and a hundred years later recusancy lists reveal strong Catholic communities at Ufton Nervet, Hampstead Norris, Buckland, Cookham, Englefield and several places in west Berkshire. During James II's reign when Catholicism again had royal approval, the Eyston's Chapel at East Hendred was refitted. But religion was one of the main causes of the abdication of James II, and a few days after William of Orange's march into England, while he was staying at Milton Manor near Abingdon, his Dutch troops billeted at East Hendred celebrated with a 'wild Popish night' and smashed the new chapel.

Non-conformists in Berkshire also suffered from persecution, particularly after the Act of Uniformity of 1662 which insisted on conformity. Twelve Berkshire clergy were ejected

61 Bray church. During the difficult years of religious changes under the Tudors the Vicar of Bray, so it was said, changed faith with each change of monarch.

from their livings in 1660, and another 12 in 1662, but many of these continued preaching, whatever the dangers. In Newbury three aldermen were also removed from office because of their beliefs. After 1672 licences to preach were issued (a useful source of revenue for the Crown), and licences were taken out in Wokingham, Maidenhead and Wallingford, and following the Toleration Act of 1689 nonconformist chapels were built in many Berkshire towns and villages.

62 *The old town hall at Newbury where nonconformists (Independents or Congregationalists) held services in 1672.*

Berkshire Levies and the Civil Wars

Today we tend to regard conscription as a 20th-century innovation, but in the Tudor times counties had long been expected to provide levies, that is, men with armour and weapons, whenever called upon. In 1513 Jack of Newbury is traditionally said to have paid for 150 men at his own expense, horsemen, pikemen and musketeers, to fight against Scotland. Usually it was the Lord Lieutenant of the county who was responsible for raising the men to fight from the parishes and towns. When Berkshire levies were called out in 1560 to fight in Scotland, a thousand men assembled at Windsor, another 1,000 at Reading and 500 at Newbury. Arms, however, it was reported, were 'scarce' and the armour had to be provided from London.

63 *The* Bear Inn *at Hungerford where Prince William of Orange met representatives of the government in 1688 on his march to London.*

64 *A soldier of a trained band, 1638.*

Berkshire also filled its quota of men to serve in Ireland in 1574 and 1581; on the latter occasion the sheriff was ordered to provide the men with coats of 'some dark and sadd colour as russet', not so light a colour as the blue and red commonly used. In 1585 and 1586, men were pressed into service to fight against Spain, and in the following year '400 able and selected soldiers' with their armour and weapons were sent to London from the Hundreds of Wantage, Lambourn, Shrivenham, Faringdon and Ganfield. Another 1,000 foot soldiers and 500 trained men were sent to fight against the Armada.

Levies were occasionally raised during the early 17th century and, as in the 16th century, lists of suitable men—muster rolls—were drawn up by the Commissioner of Array. When this was done for Berkshire in 1629, there were less than a thousand men with armour and weapons with any training. Men and money were also needed for the navy, and the illegal tax known as ship money was one of the grievances against Charles I. The Berkshire Grand Jury expressed their opposition in a petition to the King in 1640.

The inconveniences of these musters, levies and taxes, however, pales into insignificance against the misery and hardship suffered by the county during the six years of the Civil War period. At the beginning of hostilities most of the county supported the King's cause, and the towns of Abingdon, Faringdon, Reading and Wallingford were occupied by royal garrisons. From the outset, however, both Windsor and Newbury were for Parliament and, in spite of an eight-hour artillery bombardment against Windsor Castle and the two battles at Newbury, neither town was taken by the Royalists. High bulwarks and broad ditches were constructed for the defence of Reading,

65 *The Earl of Essex, Parliamentary Commander, at Windsor. On the right, pikemen can be seen parading in the Little Park.*

but in Spring 1643 after 10 days of siege by an 18,000 strong Parliamentary force, the Royalists surrendered. That same year the King appointed John Boys commander of Donnington Castle, an important stronghold guarding the western highway. In September the first of the battles of Newbury took place on Wash Common. The Parliamentary forces won the day but at a cost that could be reckoned in 50 cart loads of dead. The following year Abingdon was captured by the Parliamentary forces, and by October the year after, when the second battle of Newbury took place, most of Berkshire was under Parliamentary control.

Situated between London and the King's headquarters at Oxford, Berkshire suffered from battles and sieges, the movement of the various armies through the county, and from pillaging and the billeting of troops in private houses as well as inns and alehouses. There were gallant leaders on both sides, such as Prince Rupert and the Earl of Essex, commander at Windsor, and many stories of daring attacks, but for soldiers and residents in town and country these were years of horror and hardship, death and disease. During the early years of the war contagious diseases spread amongst the soldiers and civilian population. In some parishes, such as Sonning and Hurst, burials in 1643 were four times higher than average. A recent excavation of a cemetery at Abingdon dating from this period revealed more than 200 skeletons.

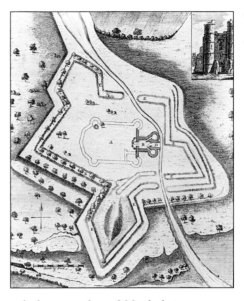

66 *Donnington Castle was a Royalist outpost during the Civil War.*

Bridges, ferries and mills along the Thames, Loddon and Kennet were broken, and trade disrupted. In 1643 Parliament assessed Berkshire as being able to pay £500 per week, and time and time again the people were expected to provide money and provisions and yet still the soldiers were not paid; starvation was a constant threat. On one occasion royalists unsuccessfully tried to commandeer five cart loads of wheat and 150 sheep from Wargrave, and on another the people of Wokingham were ordered to provide eight cart loads of bedding and firewood for the Reading garrison. At one point during the war there were 700 Roundheads billeted at Twyford.

67 *Under the command of Col. John Boyes the castle defences were substantially strengthened, and the castle withstood several assaults.*

There were numerous skirmishes at various places in the county—at Chalgrove, Harwell and Coxwell to name but three. In one way or another, few villages in Berkshire escaped from the ravages of war.

The turning point of the war came after the formation of the New Model Army which made civilians into trained soldiers. Training took place in Windsor Great Park, and in 1645 there were some ten thousand men quartered at Windsor and the neighbouring villages. Wallingford, the last of the royalist Berkshire garrisons, was taken in 1646, and Donnington Castle surrendered the same year. By July 1647 King Charles was a prisoner in Windsor Castle. That same month he was allowed to see his children for the last time at the *Greyhound Inn* at Maidenhead. However the war was not yet over, and Reading and Windsor were both used as meeting places for those who were deciding the fate of the nation. Finally in 1649 Henry Marten of Coley, a former member of Parliament for Berkshire, and Daniel Blagrave of Reading put their names to the king's death warrant and King Charles was executed in London on 29 January 1649. A few days later, on a snowy night early in February, he was secretly buried in St George's Chapel at Windsor. Berkshire had played its last part in this sorry story.

Travellers, Towns and Transport

At the beginning of the Tudor period people mainly travelled on horseback or walked, goods were carried in boats or by pack animals, and letters were sent by private messengers or by anybody going in the right direction. Two hundred years later the General Post Office had been established and there was a network of public transport by stage wagons, stage coaches and post horses, and a range of private vehicles in use from tradesmen's carts to gentlemen's carriages. The coaching era had clearly begun and the problems of the repair of the roads and the safety of travellers had already become a government concern.

The changeover from pack horses to wagons almost certainly took place gradually during the 16th century. Thomas Deloney wrote about a fictional clothier from Reading who owned so many wagons that on one occasion the king was held up for over half an hour waiting for them to pass. John Stow, author of *The Survey of London*, maintained that long wagons first began coming to London in 1564. There is little evidence to substantiate this statement, but when John Taylor compiled his *Carriers Cosmography* in 1636 there were carriers travelling once weekly between London and Abingdon, Faringdon, Reading, Tidmarsh, Wallingford and Wantage, and many more passed through the county from further west. No doubt the wagons carried a diverse range of goods, including silk stockings from Wokingham, but the most important were the bales of cloth, so much better protected in a covered wagon than in saddlebags. The carriers were unwilling to be named in John Taylor's directory for fear that the information would be used for tax purposes, but before the end of the century published descriptions of London included lists of wagons from many more

68 *Postboys were required to travel at a speed of 7 m.p.h. in summer and 5 m.p.h. in winter, and to blow their horns four times in every mile.*

places in Berkshire, including those of James Hewitt of Wokingham, Nicholas Pembroke of Swallowfield and Widow Seyward of Bradfield. John Taylor also wrote of the river trade—'the great boats that do carry and recarry passengers and goods betwixt London and the [town] of Maidenhead ... The Reading boat is to be had at Queenhithe weekly'.

Stage coach services were still in their infancy; the earliest known to travel through Berkshire was advertised in 1657. These early coaches were cumbersome vehicles, unsprung, carried only four people, and took three days to get to Bath—'God Willing'. By the late 17th century the travel time had been reduced to two days—summer weather permitting. The lists compiled by De Laune in 1681 and 1690 also listed the stage coaches services, one per day from London to Abingdon and Maidenhead, two daily coaches to Reading and no less than nine daily coach services to Windsor. There were of course coaches which travelled further afield which also served Berkshire towns.

In terms of public transport the Bristol Road (the forerunner of the A4 and more commonly known as the Bath Road) dominates the picture. It is one of only six 'post roads' established by the Tudor monarchs. The story of the postal service begins in 1511 when Henry VIII ordered Sir Brian Tuke, his new Master of Posts, to lay postal services along main roads to wherever the King was residing. By Elizabeth's reign more or less permanent arrangements had been established for the royal postal service and it was recognised that local postmasters would extend this service to members of the public. The earliest surviving accounts for the Bristol Road are dated 1579/80. The postal towns were Maidenhead, Reading and Newbury, and of these Maidenhead was clearly the most important, for the postmaster Robert Davis was paid 20d. per day while all the others along the road were paid only 12d. Later records show that this was because the Maidenhead postmaster was also responsible for the post travelling along a branch road to Oxford. When Thomas Gardener surveyed the Post Office in 1677, the Maidenhead postmaster was paid £40 per year while those of Reading and Newbury received only £30 each. By this date the Post Office had been officially opened to the public and there were post offices also at Abingdon, Faringdon and Windsor. It was common practice to use inns as post offices; in Windsor it was the *White Lion* which stood in the market place opposite the Guildhall. Letters for Wokingham arrived via Bagshot on the Exeter Road.

The increase in traffic stimulated a corresponding increase in the number of inns and alehouses serving the needs of travellers, though there are few records to chart the process. In 1577, however, proposals for a tax required Berkshire magistrates to send the names of innkeepers (as well as vintners and alehouse keepers) to the government. The figures give some evidence of the importance of the towns for travellers. The table below shows the number of inns for all places with two or more.

A few of these Elizabethan inns still exist, such as the *George* in Reading, the *Mermaid* and the *White Hart* (now known as the *Castle Hotel* and

69 *A farthing token issued by Robert Bennett, innkeeper and postmaster of Maidenhead during the 1670s; at this date there was a shortage of legal coins.*

70 Ostrich Inn *at Colnbrook. For many years landlords have been claiming it to be the third oldest public house in England, but the building is 16th century and the history of the inn has only been traced back to 1577.*

the *Harte and Garter*) in Windsor, and the *Ostrich* and the *George* inns in Colnbrook. Princess Elizabeth stayed one night at the latter *George Inn* when, as a prisoner of her sister Queen Mary, she was being taken from Woodstock to Hampton Court.

Inns in Berkshire, old and new, according to the Certificate of Inns, Taverns and Alehouses, 1577

Place	No of inns	Place	No of inns
Abingdon	9	Reading	10
Colnbrook	10	Thatcham	2
Great Faringdon	4	Tilehurst	2
Lambourn	2	Speenhamland	2
Maidenhead	3	Twyford	2
Newbury	7	Wallingford	10
New Windsor	8	Wantage	4
Wokingham	2		

There are no comparable figures for the whole county at any other dates during this period, but in 1618 Windsor had 14 inns, and 18 in 1653. In 1686, according to lists drawn up for the Secretary of State for War, there were 339 guests beds and stable room for 669 horses at Windsor's inns and alehouses. This was more than in any other Berkshire town, reflecting the needs of the Court and Castle rather than the importance of the town in any other respect. In comparison Reading had 376 beds and stabling for 572 horses. The listing was concerned with accommodation in villages as much as towns, and hamlets with only a single alehouse were included: Steventon had only one guest bed, South Moreton no beds but stabling for four horses.

The town charters granted by the Tudor monarchs mark a change in the story of Berkshire towns. Two new boroughs were created—Colnbrook and Maidenhead in 1548 and 1582 respectively. In exchange for their new status and rights to hold markets and fairs, both towns were made responsible for the maintenance of bridges on the Bristol/Bath Road. Colnbrook was still no more than an important thoroughfare village which lay in four different parishes—Horton, Iver, Langley and Stanmore. No town council ever seems to have been formed, but the surviving town records, dating from the 1620s, show the town's affairs being managed by a bridge (or chapel) warden, a highway surveyor and two rate collectors. The market was situated at the bend of the road outside the *George Inn*. In the 1590s the butchers erected their stalls so close to the inn that they impeded the passage of the inn's customers until the innkeeper, William Higgins, obtained an injunction against them.

71 *Maidenhead Borough town seal.*

Maidenhead's chief citizen was also known as a warden (instead of a mayor). Its charter established a council of 11 burgesses, two of whom were elected as bridgemen. As well as the bridges, the council was responsible for the maintenance of the town chapel and the main roads. The necessary income came from the tolls of the market and bridge and rent from town property; in the early decades of the 17th century these amounted to around £27. When the bridge was unusable, as in 1622, a ferry was provided as laid down in the charter.

Free from the control of the abbeys by their dissolution, Reading and Abingdon at last obtained the independent status for which their inhabitants had fought, and in 1596 Newbury obtained a grant of incorporation. The long established boroughs of New Windsor and Wallingford also acquired new charters with additional privileges and responsibilities. The chief citizens in these five boroughs were known as mayors and each town also had a two-tiered council made up of burgesses, brethren or aldermen (the names vary in the different towns). During their year of office the mayors were also the chief magistrates and had authority to hold borough Quarter Sessions and to appoint the necessary constables and watchmen. The councils could make bye-laws and were responsible for controlling the markets and fairs, licensing alehouses, ensuring that weights and measures were accurate and that the price and quality of ale, beer, wine and other foods were as they should be. Some retail prices and wages—maximum, not minimum—were set by statute or royal proclamation. The town crier read these out loud on market day. In Windsor the 'ancient place of proclamation' was at the crossroads where today Queen Victoria's statue stands. Numerous royal proclamations were issued every year, but in 1563 one directed at Windsor announced, amongst other things, that the maximum price for a bed for the night for one person at an inn should be one penny, and the wages of a married master carpenter no more than 12d. per day. This was a time of inflation and wages and prices were burning issues.

The original charter granted to Wokingham by Elizabeth I did not make that town a borough. Instead it confirmed that the town was still part of the manor of Sonning and came under the jurisdiction of its steward, an officer of the Crown. Its first citizen, known as the alderman, was appointed by Sonning but, with the help of two constables, two bailiffs and two aletasters, he was responsible for much of the government of the town. Not until 1612 did Wokingham get its own town council free of manorial control; the leader of the council was still to be known as the alderman, but the charter also granted the town the right to have its own town hall and town prison. Other towns also had prisons, and towns and parishes alike had their whipping posts, stocks and pillories.

Government of the county

Far more than today, the government of the county and its towns and villages in the 16th and 17th centuries lay with its chief inhabitants. The main instrument through which the law was administered were the justices of the peace, appointed by the Crown to serve a particular county. They were chosen from the county gentry, rather than nobility.

By the beginning of the 17th century there were more than three hundred statutes imposing responsibilities on the justices, more than half of them passed since the beginning of the Tudor period. Their duties were administrative and judicial, and, cajoled and scrutinised by the Privy Council, the justices were to become the effective rulers of county. In the 16th century the main business was conducted at the four general or Quarter Sessions Courts which met at Abingdon, Reading and Newbury. The Assizes met at Abingdon

72 *Village green and church, Sutton Courtenay.*

IX *Lambourn market cross.*

X *Newbury town centre.*

XI *A distant view of Didcot Power Station and Harwell Research Station.*

XII *Village cricket at West Ilsley, near Newbury.*

and Reading, but as yet neither borough was securely established as the county town. It was in order to further its claim to be the 'cheife town' that Abingdon Corporation built a county hall in the market place in 1678. Berkshire's county records were destroyed long ago but, of the many duties for which the justices were responsible, the maintenance of roads, bridges, the county prison and houses of correction, and the administration of the laws dealing with the poor, vagrancy, wages and prices and alehouse legislation are likely to have been the most important. In many parts of the country, justices also began holding local sessions to deal with much of the ordinary business and to mete out summary justice for minor offences. How soon this took place in Berkshire is not known, but the compilation of the 1577 Certificate of Inns, Taverns and Alehouses by five different groups of magistrates perhaps offers a clue as to the divisions at that date.

The justices of the peace were also responsible for overseeing the work of the parish officers—the churchwardens, overseers of the poor, highway surveyors and petty constables, and approving their accounts. The officers were unpaid, untrained and often unwilling to accept the responsibilities, and in some parishes, like Enborne, there was a rotating system so that most householders in the 'middle ranks' of the community served in their turn. Tudor laws made the parishes responsible for looking after their own poor and repairing the parish roads, and the overseers' accounts record the collection of poor rates and the disbursement of money to the needy. The homeless unemployed, however, were designated as vagrants, rogues and beggars, persons to be punished and, if able-bodied, set to work, and it was the parish constable's unpleasant duty to see that this was done. But the treatment of the poor and many other aspects of the social conditions and local law and order cannot be told in terms of laws and proclamations, for the story of every Berkshire parish is different, determined by the character of its inhabitants and those in authority over them.

Manor courts exercised control over the common fields through manor officials known probably as the bailiff and hayward, but courts were held less often than in earlier times and few now had any judicial importance. When disputes occurred over the payment of tithes, it was in the Archdeacon's Court that the matter had to be settled, and the records for the Archdeaconry of Berkshire tell the stories of numerous conflicts between villagers and tithe owners. After the Dissolution of the tiny priory at Sandleford near Newbury, the local people claimed that Sandleford was a separate parish, and for over thirty years there were annual battles in the cornfields over who had the rights to the tithe—the incumbent at Sandleford or the parson from Newbury.

In terms of law and order, the church was clearly still very important in the parishes, but no longer was it the focus and meeting place for the community as it had been. The Reformation had loosened these ties, and the tremendous increase in the number of alehouses offered a more convivial alternative. In 1577 the county had almost three hundred, with half of the parishes having at least one. The 'typical' English village with its green, church and public house in close proximity is found in books more often than in reality, but there are Berkshire examples, including West Hanney and Leckhampstead.

The Great Rebuilding

Despite the problems of poverty and inflation, the period 1570 to 1640 was also one of increased prosperity which was reflected in a wave of building and enlarging houses, from country mansions to humble farmsteads and town tenements. Windsor under the Tudors was a prosperous town; it came 32 in terms of the tax or subsidy paid by the inhabitants to the Crown in the 1520s. It was never to do so well again in comparison with other towns, and by 1662 it had sunk to 44th according to the hearth tax assessments. This waxing and waning of fortunes is reflected in the number of timber-framed buildings which survive in the centre of the town. Only a few have timbers still showing, but low ceilings and floors below street level hint at older structures hidden by brickwork and later facades. So many nobles and courtiers visited Windsor during Henry VIII's reign that in 1519 a restriction was imposed on the number of horses each visitor was allowed to bring into the town. During Elizabeth's reign the town got a new market house and for the first time the main streets were paved. Other towns were improved during this period of rebuilding, but whether or not many of the houses have survived to the present day so often depends on the subsequent history.

Visual evidence of the 'great rebuilding' can also be seen in numerous Berkshire villages. In villages such as Steventon, Childrey and Hurley, there are clusters of picturesque cottages, still resplendent in silvered timber and creamy plaster or the warm red bricks of a brick infill. Bricks were a new building material in England in the 15th century and Berkshire possesses one of the important early examples, Eton College: the oldest part was built in the 1440s with bricks made at Slough. In Tudor times, however, bricks were still a prestige material, and humbler dwellings were usually timber-framed until the second half of the 17th century. Of the buildings which then made such splendid use of bricks, Berkshire has an abundance of examples, from fine houses to public buildings such as Windsor town hall, the Kedderminster almshouses at Langley Marish, and the almshouses at Maidenhead and Bray.

Country houses 'built for the pleasure of living' originated in the 16th century; before this the need to defend the property took precedence over comfort and elegance. Shaw House and Ufton Nervet Manor House have already been mentioned. Ashdown House at Ashbury, near Lambourn, was built for the first Earl Craven about 1665 as a base for hunting on the downs; he also built a mansion at Hampstead Marshall which became his principal seat.

Unlike some counties, Berkshire does not seem to have nurtured families of the land-owning class who belonged to the county for generations; only four families

73 *Lady Place, Hurley, the seat of Lord Lovelace, the first county Lieutenant of Berkshire after the Restoration of the monarchy in 1660.*

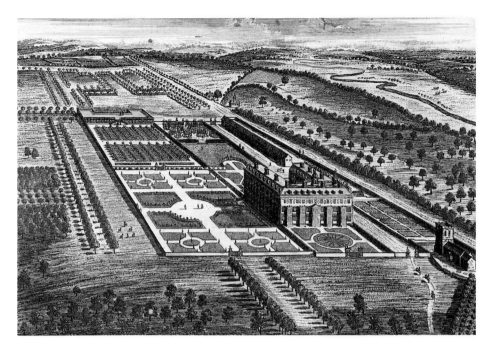

74 *Hampstead Marshall house and park, the seat of the Earl of Craven.*

who were important in the county in 1500 still had the same position on the eve of the Civil War. Recent research has shown that the proximity to London was a major factor in this fluidity in the composition of Berkshire's ruling élite. Many of the newcomers had pursued successful careers as courtiers, civil servants, lawyers or in commerce before acquiring an estate in Berkshire. For example, Sir Henry Neville, a prominent courtier in the court of Edward VI, received Billingbear Park as a gift in 1552; William Trumball, clerk of the privy council, was granted Easthampstead Park by Charles I in 1628; William Dunch, an auditor of the mint during the early 16th century, purchased several Berkshire manors; Peter Vanlore, a jewel merchant, amassed a considerable fortune supplying jewellery to the courts of Elizabeth I and James I before purchasing his first Berkshire manor—Tilehurst—in 1604.

Of the families who were prominent in the 16th century, the Essexes of Lambourn, Norreys of Wytham, Parrys of Hampstead Marshall, Untons of Wadley and Wardes of Hurst had disappeared by 1640 because of financial difficulties or the failure of the male line. Other families, such as the Fettiplaces, Darrels and Englefields, held much smaller estates than in earlier decades. Amongst those at the top of the social ladder and governing élite in the mid-17th century were the Dunches of Little Wittenham, the Knollys of Battel, and the Martens of Longworth. Through their rôle as justices of peace and sheriff, they formed a close-knit county network which in some measure influenced the affairs of the whole county. Individual members of the families often continued to be involved in professional or business activities in London and, unlike many other counties, Berkshire's gentry had close connections with the Court and Parliament throughout this period.

5

Georgian Berkshire, 1714-1837

A Royal County

Berkshire had little reason to be called a royal county during the reign of the first two Georges. Neither of the two kings stayed at Windsor Castle for more than the occasional short visit. A miscellaneous collection of people were allowed to make it their home, and itinerant tradesmen and ladies of doubtful repute sold their wares in the castle wards, and the walls facing the town were scarcely visible because of the double row of houses and shops which filled the ancient ditch. The fabric of the castle gradually fell into disrepair, and by 1775 when George III came to Windsor the royal apartments had become uninhabitable. Queen Charlotte, however, was captivated by a house in Castle Street, which the King bought and had enlarged to accommodate their large family. Windsor now became the royal family's main residence though they did not move into the castle until 1804, by which time considerable restoration had been achieved under James Wyatt.

Although the Court at Windsor was often dull and tedious, George III himself was interested in so many things. He was fascinated by architecture, and helped plan the restoration of St George's Chapel. He encouraged and financially helped William Herschel who, after leaving Bath where he had made his great discovery of Uranus, lived at Old Windsor and Datchet before settling

75 *Title page of the earliest known tourist guide to Windsor Castle. The first edition was published in 1745.*

Les Delices de Windsore;
OR, A
POCKET COMPANION
TO
WINDSOR CASTLE;
AND THE
COUNTRY ADJACENT;

Containing, a Defcription of the ROYAL APARTMENTS, and the PAINTINGS therein.

Alfo, of the ROYAL CHAPEL of St. GEORGE, and the ORDER of the GARTER; with every Particular of general Obfervation.

An Account alfo, of the TOWN, PARKS, and FOREST of WINDSOR; and the feveral VILLAGES, and GENTLEMEN'S Seats in the Neighbourhood.

To which is added, an APPENDIX;

Containing the CEREMONIES at large of the Inftallation of a KNIGHT of the GARTER:

And a Catalogue of the KNIGHTS Companions to the prefent Time.

With two Views of the CASTLE; alfo, a KNIGHT in the full Habit of the ORDER of the GARTER, and other Cutts.

The Third Edition, with the neceffary Alterations.

ETON, Printed by J. POTE, MDCCLXIX.
Sold alfo, by Mr. WALTER, Bookfeller at Charing-Crofs; Mr. FLETCHER and Co. in St. Paul's Church-Yard; Mr. PARKER, in Cornbill, London; and by J. SNOW at Windfor. (Price 2s.)

in Slough and there built his 40-inch telescope—a wonder of the world in 1789. The King's interest in agriculture led him to experiment with new methods of farming and under his direction the Flemish and Norfolk systems of crop rotation were tried out on his farms attached to the Great Park—hence their modern names. The Great Park itself was drained and its pasture brought into good condition. His nickname of Farmer George, affectionately bestowed by local people, was well deserved.

76 *The 40-inch telescope built by William Herschel at his home in Slough. It was visited by George III.*

George was also known as the Squire of Windsor, for he liked to know the tradesmen of the town, nodding to them as he walked by, and he and his wife and daughters favoured the town shops with their custom. Contemporary cartoonists such as Peter Pinder lampooned them in verse and picture:

> *Who down at Windsor daily go a-shopping*
> *Their heads, right royal, into houses popping*

Their presence, however, brought increased trade into the town and improved the quality and prices of the goods on sale. Charles Knight, bookseller, printer and future proprietor of the *Windsor and Eton Express*, compared them favourably with the best in the metropolis. No doubt he was biased, but George III's reign saw an increase in royal patronage in Windsor. In 1782 the organisation of services provided by tradesmen had been put on a more rational basis in the charge of the Lord Chamberlain; it was the beginning of the royal appointment system that we know today. One of the earliest known royal warrant holders in Windsor was Richard Martin of the *Castle Inn* who became hackney man to the King about 1784. Caley's Department Store in the High Street, which today supplies household goods to the royal family, is the direct descendant of Mrs M. Caley, dressmaker and milliner to Queen Charlotte.

Towns, Trade, Traffic and Transport

The early 18th century brought increased trade and traffic to all the towns of southern Berkshire through the growth of the coaching and carrying trade and the improved navigability of the Kennet River. Reading had long been an inland port with several wharves along the Kennet, and much of its prosperity stemmed from its trade to and from London. The main wealth of the trade, however, was now based on malting barley to make beer for the ever-growing population of London. By 1760 Berkshire had become the most important area in the country for malting and much of the wheat, barley and wood needed by Londoners came from Berkshire. Much of this was transported along the Thames via the wharves at Reading. In 1708, however, a scheme was proposed to make the river navigable as far as Newbury. Supported by towns and villages of west Berkshire and Wiltshire which expected to benefit from cheaper rates for transport of goods, it was fiercely opposed by the inhabitants of Reading—innkeepers, shopkeepers, watermen, millers and town council members—who feared a loss of custom and market tolls if businesses in the town declined. Despite their opposition the River Kennet Navigation Act was passed in 1715, and the work of canalising the river and building the 20 locks, necessary to overcome the rise of 134 feet, began. Opposition continued. A mob destroyed part of the works in 1720 and even after the navigation was opened verbal abuse and occasional violence made the journey an unpleasant and sometimes difficult operation. On one occasion, Simon Finch, the miller at Sheffield Mill at Theale, prevented barges passing through the nearby lock for eight days, and involved the owners of the mill, Reading Corporation, in a long and expensive dispute.

By 1740 the fuss was over. Reading's trade had not suffered, the economy was buoyant and road and river transport services steadily increased. New wharves were built at Newbury to serve the barges carrying coal, grocery wares, oil, tobacco and heavy goods, and the town developed a new importance serving the towns and villages of west Berkshire. The coaching trade also benefited Newbury, and in 1752 John Clark began a daily coach service from Newbury to London. The town also still had a textile industry, albeit making shalloon, a material used for linings, rather than the fine woollen cloth of earlier times. By 1740 work had begun on a new town hall.

About 1770 the Navigation Company began to study the possibilities of building a canal to link the Kennet and the Avon Rivers. Nothing came of the first proposals but in 1788 meetings were held at Hungerford to promote the scheme. A pamphlet proclaimed the advantages: cheaper carriage of coal and building materials including Bath stone, and new markets for farm produce. Farmers and estate owners would benefit as much as the towns. At first subscriptions were insufficient, but by 1792 'canal mania' had hit the country and sponsors were anxious to put up the money. Work began in 1794 and the first section between Newbury and Kintbury was opened two years later; the canal was completed in 1810. By 1818 there were more than two hundred boats using the canal, some seventy of them barges each carrying over 60 tons. Newbury had now become an important inland port, but other places also shared in the trade, and wharves were built at Hungerford and Aldermaston.

Meanwhile work had already begun on the Wilts and Berks Canal which linked the Thames at Abingdon with the Kennet and Avon Canal, with branches leading to Wantage, Longcot (for Faringdon), Calne and Chippenham. It took 16 years to construct the fifty or so miles of canal and to build the 42 locks—16 years when the Vale was noisy with the sounds of picks and shovels and the raucous voices of the navvies. The expressed purpose of the project was to bring Somerset coal to the Vale of the White Horse and to take back supplies of corn and timber, but to the north of Abingdon the area was also linked by canal to the industrial Midlands, the potteries, Birmingham and Lancashire via the Oxford and Grand Union Canals.

As elsewhere improved water transport brought increased trade to the towns served by the canals, and in 1817 a new corn market was set up in Wantage. The canals also brought a new class of people to the town—narrow boatmen and itinerant traders of all kinds including gypsies and hawkers. They dealt in cheap china, iron goods, bales of cloth as well as a miscellaneous collection of small items to attract the attention of townsfolk, farmers and villagers. They stored their wares at the wharves and used the town as winter headquarters. Some, as the parish registers testify, settled in Wantage. The impact on this small rural town was overwhelming and they contributed greatly to the growth and overcrowding of the maze of alleys and poor dwellings which lay behind the prosperous shops fronting the market square.

77 *Extract from a modern royal warrant.*

By the early 19th century Berkshire was also served by an intricate network of stage coach, stage waggon and carrier services. Evidence for the changing pattern of public transport during the 18th and early 19th centuries is too patchy to give a full picture, but advertisements and London-based lists of coaches and carriers point to a tremendous increase. At the beginning of the period only two coaches made the journey daily along the main road (A4) to Bath and Bristol, taking two days in the winter and one and a half in the summer. By the 1830s there were at least ten coaches, and the journey took only 11 hours in the fastest vehicles. Coaches travelling to other destinations also passed along the Bath Road, and in a census taken in 1834 there was a daily average of more than sixty coaches passing through Maidenhead. The earliest known coach proprietor in Berkshire was Thomas Baldwin of the *Crown Inn* in Slough who provided a daily service to Bath and Bristol in 1718. By the end of the century, if not long before, all the towns in the county were served by both stage coaches and waggons and some, like Newbury, Reading, Thatcham and Windsor, had their own companies. In the 18th century many of the stage coaches would appear to have been

78 *The* George Inn *at Colnbrook. This 16th-century inn was substantially enlarged in the 1770s and given a new façade and entrance to the inn yard. It was a mail coach stop in the 1830s.*

YE OLDE GEORGE

owned by groups of inn proprietors, but it was a very competitive business, and the subsequent history is one of mergers and failures and the development of specialist stage coach companies.

Inns were an essential link in the communication network, but which ones were used depended on the arrangements made with each stage coach company and the status of the inn. Both could and did change. In 1756 the Bath Old Machines Company advertised their new schedules and inns, naming amongst others the Windmill at Salt Hill. Fifty years later the Windmill had become far too grand to deal with stage coaches; it provided only post horses and postchaises for the gentry and nobility. Horses were changed at the stages, but not all coaches stopped at the same town, and both Colnbrook and Slough might be called the second stage out of London, Maidenhead and Twyford the third, and Reading the fourth. However, even this pattern no doubt changed during the two hundred years of the coaching era, and only one timetable is known to have survived.

Stagecoach routes through Berkshire, 1836

The number of coach services advertised in the London directories

Along the Bath and Bristol Road

London to Bath and Bristol	14
London to Newbury	1
London to Reading	2
London to Maidenhead (see below)	
London to Slough and Windsor	4
Reading to Bath	1
Reading to Newbury	2

Along the Bath Road to Maidenhead and then to Henley and elsewhere

London to Henley	1
London to Birmingham	1
London to Cheltenham & Gloucester	2
London to Hereford	1
London to Oxford	2
London to Shrewsbury	1
London to Wallingford	1
London to Abingdon & Faringdon	1
London to Stroud via Abingdon & Faringdon	1

Sixty-three daily stage coach services were advertised in the London directories for 1836 as starting, passing through or terminating in Berkshire. From the available sources of information it is difficult, and probably impossible, to reconstruct a complete picture of the routes and stages. However, the table above gives some indication of the pattern of services, though it must be remembered that not all the coaches stop in each of the towns through which they pass. There were, of course, an equal making the return journey.

The number of stage coach services passing through
Berkshire towns, 1836

Abingdon	4	Slough	35
Colnbrook	35	Reading	33
Faringdon	3	Wallingford	2
Hungerford	14	Windsor	13
Maidenhead	31	Wokingham	2
Newbury	17		

The fastest coaches were the mail coaches which began replacing the postboys on horseback along the main post roads in 1784. The first experimental run took place on 1 August that year and it is almost certain that it changed horses at the *Kings Head* at Thatcham run by Edward Fromont. Post Office records show that he provided the horses for the middle section of the mail coach route in the 1790s. Within a few years, however, the slowness of his horses had lost him the job, and the mail coaches were probably using the *George and Pelican Inn* at Speenhamland. The mail coaches delivered the mail bags only to the postal towns. The bags then had to be taken to the town post office and there sorted before the letters could be delivered by mail cart or letter carrier to lesser post offices and receiving houses. Windsor, for example, received its letters by mail carts from Staines and Maidenhead. From 1793 penny post schemes allowed delivery of letters

79 *A coach supper at the* Cross Keys *at Speenhamland, one of the inns which served the stage coach travelling along the Bath Road. From a drawing by George Cruickshank.*

80 *Timetable of Edward Fromont's stagecoach service operating from Thatcham. Superior Travelling by the Regulator, c.1830.*

STAGES.	Miles	Time allowed H.	M.	Should arrive & leave. H.	M.	STAGES.	Miles	Time allowed H.	M.	Should arrive & leave. H.	M.
1 BATH	13	1	30	6	15	1 HOUNSLOW	10	1	15	6	30
Time allowed in Ditto	....		15	6	30	2 SLOUGH............	10	1	15	7	45
2 CHIPPENHAM	13	1	35	8	5	Breakfast at the Dolphin	....		20	8	5
Breakfast at the Angel..	....		20	8	25	3 MAIDENHEAD	6		50	8	55
3 BECKHAMPTON ..	13	1	35	10	0	4 READING..........	13	1	35	10	30
4 MARLBOROUGH ..	6		50	10	50	5 THATCHAM	14	1	45	12	15
5 HUNGERFORD	10	1	15	12	5	Allowed at Ditto to change Coach ..	....		20	12	35
6 THATCHAM	12	1	35	1	40	6 HUNGERFORD	12	1	30	2	5
Allowed at Ditto to change Coach ..	....		20	2	0	7 MARLBOROUGH ..	10	1	15	3	20
7 READING..........	14	1	45	3	45	Dine at the Castle	....		40	4	0
Dine at the Bear	....		45	4	30	8 BECKHAMPTON ..	6		50	4	50
8 MAIDENHEAD	13	1	40	6	10	9 CHIPPENHAM	13	1	35	6	25
9 SLOUGH............	6		50	7	0	10 BATH	13	1	35	8	0
10 HOUNSLOW	10	1	15	8	15	Allowed in ditto	....		15	8	15
11 HATCHETT's HOTEL	10	1	15	9	30	11 BRISTOL	13	1	30	9	45
	120	16	45				120	16	30		

to many smaller villages at an extra cost of a penny. Berkshire had seven post or sub-post towns (eight if one includes Colnbrook), each with a number of receiving houses:

81 *The Colnbrook Penny Post. This sketch was drawn by the Post Office surveyor in 1813 to show the route of the foot postman.*

Abingdon	3	Colnbrook	3	Faringdon	1	Maidenhead	6
Newbury	7	Reading	4	Wallingford	3	Windsor	3

Most people, however, still had to collect their letters from the office, be it in village or town, since delivery to every household did not become an accepted right until Queen Victoria's Diamond Jubilee in 1897. In the postal towns, such as Reading, Newbury and Windsor, letters were delivered without extra charge to houses within the town boundaries— a situation which inevitably led to disputes as the towns grew, and occupiers of new houses outside the boundaries were charged an extra penny. Post Office archives contain numerous records of such disputes, including the correspondence from Captain Oke of Clarence Road,

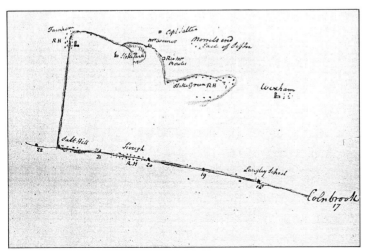

Windsor, as well as maps showing extensions to the free postal areas of Reading and Newbury.

82 *Turnpike Trust milestone at Twyford.*

Mud and Ruts, and the battle of the wheels

The system of road maintenance set up by the Tudor Highway Acts could not cope with the effects of this tremendous increase in traffic. It was the statutory duty of each parish to keep in good repair all the public roads within its boundaries, but it was impossible for parishes with small populations to provide either the manpower or the money to look after main highways used by through traffic. The idea that tolls collected from travellers using the road could be used for road maintenance was tried out on the North Road in Hertfordshire in the 1670s, and then revived in the early 18th century as the need for improved roads became essential. Local landowners and men of influence combined to set up turnpike trusts (sanctioned by local Acts of Parliament) to take over the maintenance of particular stretches of the main roads. The first two Berkshire trusts were formed in George I's reign; they became responsible for the Bath Road from Maidenhead to Twyford, and Reading westwards to Puntfield near Theale. The last part of the Bath Road through Berkshire to be turnpiked was the stretch immediately east of Reading. This was partly because the terrain was good, but also because of opposition to any road improvements which might jeopardise Reading's water transport. Crossing the county from east to west, travellers now had to pass through at least seven turnpike gates, paying a toll at each.

Turnpiking a road, however, did not necessarily mean a great improvement to the road surface, since the principles of road maintenance were not yet understood. A description published in the *Gentleman's Magazine* in

83 *Turnpike Trust pump erected for laying the dust.*

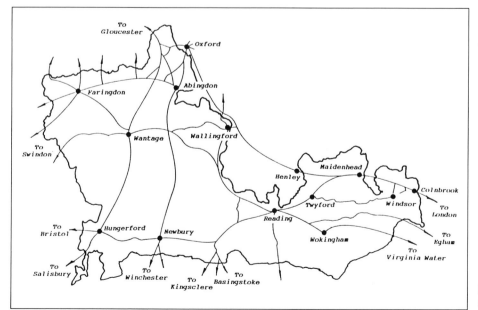

84 *The turnpike roads of Berkshire, c.1800.*

85 *Turnpike gate and toll collector's cottage at Eddington, c.1850.*

1754 perhaps exaggerates, but other contemporary descriptions testify to the inadequacies of the work of the turnpike trusts:

> ... that great road from London to Bath; it errs and blunders in all the forms; its strata of materials were never worth a straw; its surface was never made cycloidal; it hath neither good side ditches, nor foot paths for walkers; no outlets were made for water that stagnates in the body of the road; it was never sufficiently widened, nor were the hedges ever cleared. Of course 'tis the worst public road in Europe, considering what vast sums have been collected from it.

The government passed numerous Acts in an attempt to deal with the problem of the roads, but its efforts were directed at the wheels and weights of the vehicles, not the roads themselves and, although undoubtedly roads did improve during the 18th century, they could and did become impassable at times. It was not until the early 19th century that Thomas Telford and John Louden McAdam put forward their ideas on road construction. McAdam's techniques not only ensured a good road surface which was improved by the passage of vehicles, but cost less than the old methods. Within a few years trusts all over the country were employing members of the McAdam family and putting the improvements into operation, including at least seven in Berkshire: the Chilton to Andover, the Fyfield to Abingdon, the Fyfield to St Johns Bridge, the Hurley, the Maidenhead, the Newbury, and the Reading Turnpike Trusts. George Botham of the *George and Pelican Inn* at Speenhamland and Edward Fromont of the *Kings Head* at Thatcham both testified at a Parliamentary enquiry in 1819 as to the road improvements brought about by McAdam.

The last of the Berkshire turnpike trusts was founded as late as 1832. Unlike most of the earlier trusts, which were mainly responsible for the improvement of already established roads, the Windsor to Twyford trust was

concerned at the outset with the construction of a new length of road—
the eastern end of the modern B3024
out of Windsor. Most roads, however, were still the responsibility of
the parishes, and the post of parish
highway surveyor was still served by
untrained and unpaid local inhabitants. Aldermaston ratepayers were
fined in 1760 for neglect of duty.
Statutory labour (that is unpaid
labour by householders) had long
been replaced by the payment of
highway rates, but in many parishes
the work of breaking stones and fill-
ing potholes, clearing ditches and
smoothing out the ruts was done by
the poor of the parish for a mini-

mum wage. It was a way of trying to solve two of the most trying problems
confronting parish vestries—maintaining the poor and the roads. As the
assistant-overseer to the parish of Windsor explained in 1833 to His Majesty's
Commissioners during their enquiry about the administration of the Poor
Laws, 'We have no labour to give our paupers but work on the roads'. It was
a remark echoed by many other parish officers in the county.

86 *A cartoon of 1817 showing John McAdam as the colossus controlling the Great North Road and the Great West Road.*

Poverty—the growth of pauperism

By the 18th century the tramping poor—the homeless and unemployed, the
rogues, vagabonds and sturdy beggars as they were referred to in so many
laws and pamphlets—were no longer a regular sight on the main roads and
in the alehouses. The Poor Laws had made it more difficult for people to
travel in search of work and to get help from a parish in which they did not
have legal settlement. Hundreds of examination and settlement certificates
and removal papers survive amongst the Quarter Sessions records and allow us to catch a glimpse of a system at work which encouraged parish
officers to take before the local magistrates any newcomer to the village who
became, or might become, a charge on the rates, and have him or her and
their family removed. Parishes were only responsible for looking after their
own poor, and it was the responsibility of the magistrates to examine the
paupers and find out where they were legally settled, that is, where they had
been born or had been employed for a whole year. Vagrant passes or certificates signed by the county treasurer authorised payment to the constables for the conveying of paupers across the county. A bundle of these
passes found amongst the Buckinghamshire Quarter Sessions records gives
some idea of the numbers of families involved. During the last three months
of 1752, Caesar Willis, the constable at Colnbrook, was required to take by

cart, on average 12 times per week, families and individuals to Maidenhead—one step on their journeys to as far afield as Bristol, Wales, Ireland, Gloucester, Herefordshire. It was a harsh and expensive way to deal with the problems of poverty and an unpleasant and onerous task for the magistrates and parish constables.

Not all the poor, who for one reason or another found themselves in difficulties, were so harshly treated. In a few parishes, such as Barkham, a kindly and benevolent parson like the Rev. David Davis (1742-1819) operated a paternalistic relief system, caring as well as he could for the poor of the parish. Long Wittenham parish owned 18 cottages which were let out rent free to poor parishioners, and several other parishes, such as Woodley, Langley, Chalvey, Eton, and Wantage, had poor houses or workhouses where the destitute could find refuge. The Wantage overseers regularly paid out considerable weekly sums, and the accounts show payments for shoes, clothing, medicines, and shaving for the inmates of its workhouse.

Some parish authorities were neither kindly nor conscientious. The autobiography of Charles Knight Jnr. tells of a very mis-organised parish system at Windsor. Most officers, he wrote, were content to remain in ignorance of how the poor rate money was spent, leaving it to the discretion of an assistant overseer of the poor who gave or denied relief to the needy according to their 'character': 'With him squalid filth was a test of destitution' and 'whining gratitude' a measure of the deserving poor. None of the officers, nor the vicar or curates, had any conception of the real living conditions of the 150 or so recipients of weekly relief. At Eton the town inhabitants had to take Eton College to court in order to make the College authorities pay rates on houses they owned in the town, and the overseers could only afford to pay 2s. a week to wives and families of militiamen serving in the army—scarcely enough to pay for a diet of bread. At Reading, according to a contemporary comment, the poor houses were filled to overflowing and the overseer's door was 'surrounded from morning to night by miserable objects seeking relief'.

Wages for artisans and tradesmen had risen so that many were able to maintain themselves and their families on what they earned in half a week—leaving something to spend for pleasure or to save. But, as Davis commented in his book, *The Case for Labourers in Husbandry*, most country labourers in the 1790s could not earn enough in a whole week to maintain their families for more than four or five days. Agricultural wages in Berkshire were amongst the lowest in the country and, as Davis knew from his own experience at Barkham, the day labourer with his 'utmost exertions ' could scarcely supply their families with daily bread, and the women spent much time in tacking their tattered and ragged garments together, and there was nothing left over unless the wife and children worked. According to Davis the number of poor receiving relief had tripled since the beginning of the century, and such was the burden on the small number of ratepayers in some parishes that the overseers of the poor were forced to reject many of the claims.

In the last decades of the 18th century conditions went from bad to worse. There were several years of bad harvests, and corn was both scarce and costly. Inflation was severe and rates almost doubled (from 2s. in the £ in 1780 in Barkham to 3s. 6d. in 1800). Labourers' wages were kept to the minimum, and there were bread riots in Newbury in 1766, at Thatcham in 1800, and Windsor in 1804. Bread became so expensive that in the 1790s Berkshire magistrates circulated the suggestion that every parish should appropriate a few acres for growing potatoes to make potato bread. Taxes imposed on malt in aid of the French War, and the suppression of alehouses made beer a luxury, unobtainable for many. In April 1795 at the Quarter Sessions held at the *George and Pelican Inn* at Speenhamland, the Berkshire magistrates decided on a scale of relief based on the price of bread and the size of the family. This became known as the Speenhamland System and was adopted by parishes all over the country. Poor rates became a substitute for fair wages—a 'miserable substitute' providing 'little that belly can spare for the back'. It was an ill-conceived system which pauperised the labourers and corrupted their employers. The Rev. Thomas Whately of Cookham (1797-1837), amongst others, was very much against it and strove to help the labourers of his parish to become self-supporting. He reduced the amount of financial help given to unmarried mothers, thus substantially decreasing the number of illegitimate births and the money paid out in relief. He also founded a voluntary benevolent fund and a very successful penny-a-week saving scheme.

Conditions worsened in the early decades of the 19th century, affecting shops and businesses as well as the poor. In 1812, according to the *London Gazetteer*, there was a great increase in the number of bankruptcies. One of these was the tannery at Wantage, ' the largest and most up-to-date in the Kingdom', according to William Mavor, a government inspector; it was worth more than £8,000 and occupied almost a third of the town. More important, it was the biggest employer of labour in Wantage, and its downfall also brought about the failure of other local firms, such as that of Maurice Blackford, shoemaker, and John House, currier (leatherworker), and the loss of employment for a large number of Wantage labourers and skilled workers. Other Berkshire towns also suffered financial disasters, and deprivation stalked hand-in-hand with the emergence of the modern consumer society.

The County at war—military and militia

England was at war for much of the 18th century, and year after year Parliament passed Acts which allocated funds for a specified number of soldiers, and confirmed the use of inns and alehouses for their quarters. Men were actively encouraged to volunteer and 'take the King's shilling' during the Jacobite rebellion of 1715, at the outbreak of the Seven Years War in 1756, and for the French (Napoleonic) War at the end of the century. In 1782, the 66th Regiment of Foot, which had been formed at the beginning of the Seven Years War, added the name Berkshire to its name, and became affiliated to the county. In 1792 an immense tented camp was established for a short time near Caesar's camp in Easthampstead parish, and here some 7,000 soldiers, including the Berkshire regiment, received training and the men took part in the earliest known organised military manoeuvres. The event attracted enormous national interest with regular reports in the newspapers and large crowds of spectators. In the Peninsular War its 2nd Battalion served under Sir Arthur Wellesley (later the Duke of Wellington) with great distinction and earned nine battle honours. Later they were responsible for guarding the deposed Emperor Napoleon on St Helena, and Grenadiers from the 66th were among those that bore his body to the grave.

Quite separate, but equally important were the county militia. They were the county's home guard and emergency police. Fear of invasion and the importation of Hanoverian troops by George II led to the re-establishment and reform of the militia system in 1757. Recruitment in Berkshire was the responsibility of George Beauclerk, the 3rd Duke of St Albans and Lord Lieutenant of the county. An Act of Parliament dictated the number of men each county was to provide; the quota for Berkshire included 565 rank and file. The provision of horses, arms and men became the statutory duty of every parish, and in July 1757 the Berkshire bands (that is the groups of conscripted men from the parishes) were amongst the first to be embodied under the new regulations. The militia men were chosen by lot and compelled to serve for three years or to provide £10 for a substitute; the parish raised a rate to pay for the required number of men and equipment. When Newbury could not provide six men in 1796, the parish was fined £210 and the money was raised by a rate of 10d. in the pound.

The militia were not a full-time force, but were expected to train for two or three weeks each year and to turn out when called. The full force of 30 sergeants, 20 drummers and 560 rank and file were first called out for

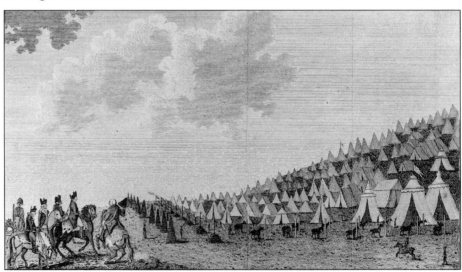

87 *View of the military camp at Wickham Bushes in Easthamstead Parish, 1792. George III and other members of the Royal Family were frequent visitors.*

duty at Hungerford, Marlborough and Devizes in July 1759 when there was fear of a French invasion. The militia were also called out to quell a bread riot at Newbury in 1766. Two-thirds of the Berkshire militia were called out in 1792 for home defence, and during 1794-1795 they contributed to the defensive cordon along the southern coast. The militia were primarily an infantry force, but there was also a conscripted cavalry militia regiment known as the Berkshire Provisional Cavalry.

In 1793, when France declared war, the government realised that the militia would be inadequate to resist a French invasion, and an Act was passed which permitted the raising of volunteer corps, infantry and cavalry, under the county lord lieutenants. Infantry volunteers were mainly drawn from the ranks of unskilled workers and artisans; cavalry recruits came from farmers' and tradesmen's families, and officers were the gentlemen of the county. The first mounted troop to be formed in Berkshire was the Abingdon Independent Cavalry. The second troop, the Woodley Cavalry, was formed in 1798; it was commanded by Captain Henry Addington, Speaker of the House of Commons, who owned Woodley Lodge. By June that year four other mounted troops had been raised at Newbury, Thatcham, Hungerford and Maidenhead. The following year the whole of the Berkshire Volunteer Corps, cavalry and infantry, were reviewed by George III at Bulmershe Heath. Two more troops were formed in 1800—the Loyal Windsor Cavalry and the Wargrave Rangers. That year for the first time the yeomanry were used as a police force when the Thatcham Volunteer Cavalry were called out by the local magistrates because some four hundred people had assembled in Thatcham demanding an increase in farm labourers' wages or cheaper food. They were to be used on eight other occasions during the next fifty years before the county constabulary was formed.

In 1804 several of the troops were formed into the 1st Regiment of the Berkshire Cavalry under the command of Lt. Col. Charles Dundas of Kintbury, MP for Berkshire, and an attempt was made to regiment the other troops, mainly in the eastern part of the county, but without success. In 1805 George III once again inspected the Berkshire Yeomanry and Infantry corps on Bulmershe Heath. It was a spectacular occasion with over a thousand volunteers from all over Berkshire, some of whom had taken two days to march there, and over twenty-thousand spectators enjoying the colour and noise of marches, manoeuvres and military bands. Patriotic feelings ran high. Charles Knight wrote that the chief business of Windsor life at this date was the volunteer drills and reviews. Thrice-weekly attendance was compulsory for those who had joined the Windsor Corps and there were hours of preparation work before an officer could be properly dressed for the part. In 1828 the volunteer troops were disbanded as one of the government's measures to reduce public expenditure—but only three years later the officers were asked to re-raise their troops because of the agriculture riots of the previous year. Eventually they became the Royal Berkshire Yeomanry, a regiment which not only served bravely as part of the country's fighting force, but played an important rôle in the county's social life.

The Napoleonic wars lasted over twenty years, and for much of this time there was a fear of invasion, but for most inhabitants the most immediate evidence of the war came in the form of taxes and rates, and the pitiful sight of crippled soldiers returning from the war. Occasionally also the neighbourhood would be filled with regular soldiers or militia when they were quartered in the inns and alehouses. How often this occurred has not been ascertained, but war office records contain bundles of petitions against the practice, including one from Twyford, dated January 1800, in which the victuallers complained that 28 men and 27 horses were quartered in the village, and that in consequence their regular customers had been turned away. The licensees had also been driven to the necessity of hiring stables at their own expense to accommodate the horses.

Between 1808 and 1811 Reading was made the home of a contingent of more than two hundred Danish and Norwegian prisoners of war. These were mainly officers and, being on parole rather than prisoners, they lived in private lodgings and enjoyed the social life of the town. A stone memorial on the wall of St Mary's Church is a lasting reminder of this event in Reading's history, but south of Windsor in the Great Park is a rather more beautiful memorial to 18th-century soldiers—Virginia Water. It was created by the Duke of Cumberland, George II's son, when he was Ranger in the 1750s. He used soldiers disbanded after Culloden, including Hanoverian mercenaries, to do much of the manual work. The military academy at Sandhurst also owes its existence to this period. It was founded by General le Marchant, who believed that promotion for officers should depend on ability, not on rank and seniority.

88 *Sandhurst College; cadets can be seen taking part in sports in the mid-ground of the picture.*

The Countryside Transformed

On 5 May 1762 a group of Englefield farmers, tenants of the manor and owner occupiers, signed an agreement to suspend their customary ways of farming the Great Field for seven years. This field and the much smaller Puntfield, and the common meadow known as Englefield Mead, were the last remnant of the old open fields left in the parish. Enclosure by agreement had long been practised in the county and was responsible for the disappearance of open fields from many parishes, such as Waltham St

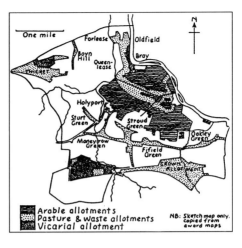

89 *Land enclosed in Bray Parish under the 1786 Enclosure Act.*

Lawrence in 1596/7, Hadley and Cobindon in Lambourn in 1614, Donnington Field in Shaw, and Marcham in 1714. But although the more progressive members of a parish might be in favour of the consolidation of their scattered strips in the open fields and the enclosure of the commons, others were unconvinced or fearful of such change. In such circumstances, if enclosure was to be achieved, it had to be done through a private Act of Parliament. Over a hundred such Acts were passed, each dealing with an individual Berkshire parish, the majority taking place during the French wars when propaganda proclaimed enclosure a patriotic measure.

Sometimes, such as at Bray, there was more than one Act; the earliest dated 1786 only involved common arable fields and a relatively small number of the landowners, while the Act of 1814 dealt with the remainder of the open fields and the several greens and areas of common pasture and involved more than 200 landowners.

There were 131 dissenters against this Act, but they owned insufficient land to prevent the Bill being passed and here, as elsewhere in the county, enclosure wrought a transformation of the landscape. Small fields surrounded by hedgerows with trees replaced the great open fields, the village greens and the large stretches of heath and common. Bulmershe Heath disappeared in 1820 and Mortimer Common in 1804. The Windsor Forest Inclosure Act was passed in 1813, and soon after that the forest legally ceased to exist. The Crown's forest rights were extinguished at the same time as the usual common rights, and

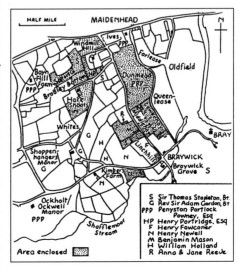

90 *Land enclosed in Bray Parish under the 1814 Enclosure Act.*

91 *The Eton banner used to celebrate the defeat of the Eton Enclosure Bill in 1826.*

in each parish the Crown was awarded a substantial allotment. Where this land was planted with trees, as in the area to the south west of Windsor, Windsor Forest became a reality in a rather different way with the creation of new woodlands.

The enclosure and re-allotment of the land brought great benefits to many people in Berkshire. Landowners were able to increase the rents for farms whose land was enclosed, and farmers could more easily improve yields by making use of new agricultural machinery and improved strains of seed and animals. Extinguishing the common rights also meant that a land-owner could now do as he wished with his own land, including turning it into residential land. Mortimer Common is just one example of a village which came into existence as an indirect result of enclosure.

Most villagers, however, did not own their cottages and so were not entitled to any compensation for their loss of rights to put a cow or goose on the common, or to take turf or wood for fuel. Enclosure also put an end to the time-honoured custom of squatting on the waste land—building a simple house and claiming a small area for a garden. The Windsor Forest Inclosure Commissioners found dozens of such closes, including several on Ascot Heath and at Bearswood. In almost every parish villagers lost much of their independent status.

92 *Berkshire Nott Wether sheep.*

Enclosure was only one of the many changes taking place during this period of agricultural improvement. New varieties of corn and root vege-tables, and improved breeds of livestock were introduced, as well as new farming practices and types of machinery. One of the most remarkable agricultural pioneers, Jethro Tull, was the son of a Berkshire farmer at Basildon. Tull practised his improved methods of sowing seeds and cultivat-ing the land on his farm at Crowmarsh near Wallingford and then on his hill farm in the parish of Shalbourne. He invented a horse-drawn seed drill (rather than sow broadcast), but it was the success of his horse-drawn hoe which led him to publish *The New Horse Hoeing Husbandry* in 1731 which eventually led to increased and improved yields. The Berkshire pig, a large black-skinned animal, was developed by the farmers of the Wantage and Faringdon area. The Hampshire Down sheep was bred from three breeds including the Berkshire Knott. It was eminently suitable for keeping on the Berkshire downs in sheep folds and being fed on root crops and oilseed cake in fields which would later be used for growing corn. William Humphreys of Oak Ash near Newbury was one of the farmers involved in determining the characteristics of the Hampshire Down breed.

For the farmers and landowners in general these new ideas could mean increased yields, profits and rents but, as in more modern times, improved efficiency did not always also benefit the workers. Increased use of labour-saving machines, especially threshing machines, brought a loss of employ-ment, particularly during the winter months when threshing had been done by hand. Hostility and desperation came to a head in 1830 and much of southern England experienced what has been called the 'last labourers' revolt' or the Swing riots. Captain Swing was the name used on hundreds of threat-

93 *Berkshire pig.*

ening letters. In Berkshire, protest started peacefully with several hundreds of workers meeting at Thatcham on 15 November, but on the following day and during the rest of the week the demonstrators visited farms in Bucklebury, Bradfield, Stanfield Dingley, Beenham, Aldermaston and Brimpton, destroying some thirty threshing machines and burning haystacks and ricks. At Brimpton the men were met by a force of constables, gentry, farmers and labourers, under the command of a justice of the peace, the Rev. Cove, and 11 men were arrested. Troubles continued and the next week a company of Grenadier Guards and a detachment of dragoons were sent to Newbury to assist local militia to round up suspected rioters who were taken to Newbury and then to Reading gaol. There were also incidents at Burghfield, Hurst, Ashampstead, Streatley, Yattendon and Basildon. Altogether 138 Berkshire men were tried at the Quarter Sessions Courts at Reading and Abingdon. Of these 59 were acquitted or discharged, 45 transported, and one man—William Winterbourne of Kintbury—was hanged.

94 *Jethro Tull, one of the foremost 18th-century agricultural pioneers, son of a farmer at Basildon. He farmed at Crowmarsh and Shalbourne.*

95 *Sheep being folded on the Berkshire Downs near West Ilsley. Moving the hurdles each day was labour intensive work.*

96 *Whiteknights house and park, seat of Sir Henry Englefield, 1776.*

97 *Basildon house and park.*

The labourers' protest was uncoordinated and achieved little direct success, but out of it grew the Windsor and Wokingham Forest Associations for the Prosecution of Felons and the Royal South Bucks Agricultural Society (covering the Slough area), which aimed at improving the relationship between the farmers and the workers.

The 18th century brought another great change in the countryside with the growth of the fashion for landscaped gardens and parks. The most celebrated was probably Whiteknights at Earley, which was owned by the Marquis of Blandford (later the fifth Duke of Marlborough) in the early 19th century. The gardens and conservatories contained numerous examples of rare and exotic plants and captured the interest of the royal family.

Other parks which were remodelled during this period include Basildon and Woodley Lodge Mansion which was landscaped by Humphry Repton for Henry Addington, when he owned the property in the late 18th century, and then 'restored' by John Louden and renamed Bulmershe Court. Great houses, such as Basildon Park, were rebuilt in the fashionable classical style, but as in earlier centuries the great landowning families did not settle for long in the county, and the history of most of these houses is one of changing owners and tenants.

The Age of Reform

At this period, as for many years earlier, the government of the county was in the hands of the justices of the peace but, unlike most other counties, Berkshire had two, not one, county towns—Abingdon and Reading. The Assize Court and Quarter Sessions Courts met in both towns. The county gaol was at Reading but both had a house of correction (or bridewell) which was used for detaining offenders from various parts of the county as well as from the two towns.

The last quarter of the 18th century saw a considerable increase in the activities of the Quarter Sessions Court, and in particular the improvement of the prisons. This was partly the result of a prison reform movement, though overcrowding and improved security were also important considerations. Reading gaol was enlarged in 1768 and again in 1775, and then rebuilt in 1794; a new bridewell was erected in 1786. Abingdon's bridewell was rebuilt between 1804 and 1818. With cells for 32 prisoners, courtyards, day rooms for different types of prisoners, a chapel, two infirmaries, a court room and accommodation for the keeper, it was the largest single building operation yet carried out by the Berkshire Quarter Sessions. During the forty years from the early 1780s to the 1820s county expenditure increased nearly five times and, although the upkeep of bridges, the maintenance of militiamen's families and the passage of vagrants were major costs to the county, during some years as much as a third of the county money was expended on the prisons and associated considerations.

98 *Disputes over the responsibility for the repair of bridges were not unusual, especially when it involved two counties. This print shows Caversham Bridge being built half in stone and half in wood.*

The last two decades before the Victorian period saw the passing of a sheaf of Acts of Parliament which brought far-reaching changes to the counties. The Test and Corporation Acts were repealed in 1828, which meant that no longer would nonconformists be barred from holding municipal offices. Soon after this date William Heelas, a staunch member of the Baptist Church, was elected alderman at Wokingham. The following year the Catholic Emancipation Act removed discrimination against Roman Catholic schools, and within a year Baylis House School had been opened at Slough. An Education Act of 1833 allowed the government for the first time to make grants to schools for improvements to buildings. Until this date education had not been the concern of either national or local government, and it was still mainly in the hands of the churches, charities and private individuals.

The Reform Act of 1832 extended Parliamentary franchise to freeholders and householders of property in the rural areas rated at a moderate value, a measure which gave the vote to 'middle class' men on the principle that such men would have the welfare of the community at heart. Annual lists of electors have not survived for Berkshire, but those for the parishes which were once part of Buckinghamshire are still amongst the county records. In the parish of Upton cum Chalvey, which included the villages of Chalvey and Upton as well as the new town of Slough, only about 57 men out of 936—that is six per cent—had a vote in 1851. The property qualification meant that a man who owned property in two or more constituencies had a vote in each of them. One such resident of Upton was James Bedborough, a master builder whose business premises were in Windsor.

99 *The old town hall and market place at Wokingham.*

Berkshire was represented by three members of Parliament; in 1832 these were R. Palmer, Philip Pusey and Viscount Barrington. The county was divided into four polling districts, and any elector wishing to vote had

to travel to the nearest hustings at Abingdon, Faringdon, Maidenhead, Wokingham, Newbury, Reading, or East Ilsley. There was as yet no secret ballot, and each elector had to register his vote with the official—to the approval or disapproval of the crowd. The four towns of Abingdon, Reading, Wallingford and New Windsor also each sent two members to Parliament. Towns such as Newbury had long since lost this right.

The Municipal Corporations Act of 1835 abolished the ancient self-perpetuating town corporations and replaced them by elected town councils and gave the vote in local elections to all ratepayers who had lived in the town for three years. In Berkshire the Act applied to Abingdon, Maidenhead, Newbury, New Windsor, Reading, and Wallingford, but Wokingham seems to have been overlooked and its old, self-perpetuating Corporation persisted under its 1612 charter.

The Tithe Act was passed in 1836. Payment of tithes to lay tithe-owners had been a contentious issue for a long time, but improvements in agriculture had aggravated the situation because increased yields meant higher tithe payments. The Act did not abolish tithes, but commuted them to a money rent based on average payments for the previous seven years. In parish after parish meetings were held, the land surveyed and the tithe commissioners did their work. There were some disputes, but not many, and by 1852 the Act had been implemented. In contrast the Poor Law Amendment Act of 1834, although implemented almost as quickly, stirred up a considerable amount of controversy and brought into being a new type of workhouse which was to be such a feature of Victorian England.

6

The Victorian Era, 1837-1901

God's Wonderful Railway

Perhaps more than any other invention it is the railway which symbolises the Victorian period. It altered the pace of life, opened up the country for trade and leisure pursuits, and influenced the lives of both rich and poor in a wide variety of ways. Berkshire was one of the first counties to be affected by the new mode of travel. Proposals for a railway line from London to Bristol were being discussed as early as 1824, and the Great Western Railway Bill received the royal assent in 1835. By 1838 the line was open as far as Maidenhead and three years later Bristol celebrated the completion of the whole line.

Support for the railway had come from many local businessmen and the corporations of such towns as Reading who could envisage the advantages. But there was also considerable opposition. Farmers and landowners, such as Robert Palmer of Sonning, an MP for Berkshire, were on the whole against the schemes, as were the *Berkshire Chronicle*, and the people with an interest in road, river and canal transport. Maidenhead Corporation opposed the scheme until compensation had been agreed for the loss of bridge tolls. Initially Windsor Corporation had been keenly interested in the railway, but when it became clear that no line would reach the town, the Council became angry and bitterly anti-railway. The strongest opposition, however, came from Eton College which feared that the railway would 'materially endanger the discipline of the School'. Such was the influence of the College that the Great Western Railway Act included a clause which forbade the building of a railway station within three miles of the College. Accordingly the station which served this stretch of the line was built at Langley, but when the line opened in June 1838 the train stopped at Slough (no more

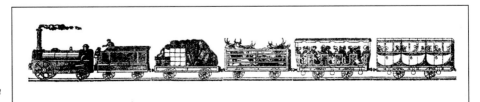

100 *Great Western Railway train.*

than two miles from Eton) without
the benefit of platform or station;
Langley Station remained unused for
eight years.

The line west of Reading did not
follow the route of the Bath Road, but
instead swung north, passing through
Pangbourne, Goring and Didcot, en
route for Bath and Bristol. The Kennet
Valley branch line which served
Newbury and Hungerford was not
constructed until 1847 and stopped at

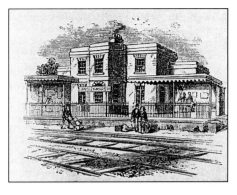

101 *Langley station:
built for the opening of
the line in 1838 but not
used until 1846.*

Great Bedwyn just over the county boundary. Two years later the Reigate
to Guildford, Wokingham and Reading line was built, and the completion
of the GWR branch from Slough to Windsor and the South Western Railway line from Waterloo to Windsor brought an end to some of the 'most
bitter conflicts' in railway history.

During the next ten years, other lines were built in Berkshire, including
the branch lines from Twyford to Henley, Maidenhead to Marlow and High
Wycombe, and Reading to Wokingham. But the optimism which prompted
so much railway building was not always rewarded, and the lines through
Wokingham were never profitable. Later in the century Newbury became a
minor railway centre with the construction of lines to Didcot (1882), to
Winchester (1885) and to Lambourn (1898), the last line to be built in
Berkshire.

The impact of the railways on Victorian Berkshire was revolutionary
in many senses of the word. With picks, shovels, horse and cart, and gun-
powder, gangs of navvies wrought a considerable change on the landscape—

102 *Didcot station,
c.1850, as illustrated in*
Measome's *Guide to the
Great Western Railway.*

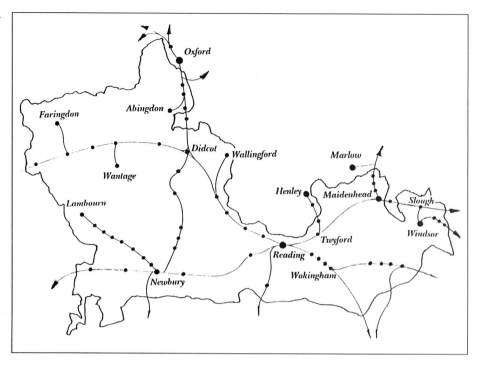

iron roads so level that in the case of the Great Western line it was nick-named 'Brunel's billiard table', embankments, bridges, new roads, and, most impressive of all, the Sonning cutting which took three years to complete. At its greatest extent, there were railway stations in more than fifty Berk-shire villages and towns. Some, like Reading, Windsor and Slough, were a credit to Victorian design and engineering. Reading's station is the original built for Brunel, but the others were built towards the end of the 19th century. As late as 1892, however, the people of Thatcham were forced to use a wooden station that had been described as ' a wooden shanty', and gave little protection from the weather. Newbury's station was described by one discontented passenger as an 'undersized chicken coop'.

If some of the original fears of the landowners were never realised, others certainly were, and several farms and estates suffered a loss of good agricultural land. Slough Farm was separated from many of its fields by the line, and before the end of the century the farm had been lost, the victim of the railway and the expansion of the brick-making industry. So much common land was taken from the parish of Eton for the great sweep of the branch line from Slough to Windsor that the Great Western Railway had to pay compensation to the commoners. Eventually this money was used to provide recreation grounds in Eton town and the village of Eton Wick. In Windsor, on the other hand, the compensation money paid by the South Western Railway Company was used to improve the environs of the castle. Houses which had been built in the castle ditch were bought and demolished

and the ancient Little Park was enlarged and renamed the Home Park.
The Datchet Bridge was demolished
and replaced by two new bridges
served by a new road system paid for
by the railway company. Within the
centre of the town the construction of
the Great Western Railway station had
meant the demolition of the town gaol
and houses in George Street. This was
one of the worst streets in the town
for vice and appalling living conditions, but no compensation or alternative accommodation was offered at
all to those who lost their homes.

The effect of the railway on Berkshire's towns and villages shows a fas-
cinating diversity. The inhabitants of
places such as Newbury, Thatcham,
Twyford, Theale and Hungerford,
whose main trades had been dependent upon road, or road and water

104 *Wantage tramway notice.*

transport, no doubt watched the progress of the railway with unease. They
had good reason, for within a few years the long distance coaching and
carrying services were ended and many of the coaching inns were either
closed or demoted to being merely public houses. The prestigious *George and
Pelican* at Speenhamland, the *Crown* and the *Bear* at Reading, and the *Castle*
at Salt Hill were all closed before the end of the 1840s. It now took less than
an hour to get from north-west Berkshire to London instead of five hours by
stage coach. Long distance stage waggons and carriers also ceased operating
and the turnpike companies were soon in financial difficulties. Profits of the
Windsor Forest Turnpike declined from £743 in 1844 to £414 in 1850, just
one year after the railway line reached Wokingham. By 1870 all the turnpike
trusts had been closed and the repair of the roads was neglected.

The railway was also in direct competition with the canals, and the
prosperous years for the canal companies were over. From 1847 heavy goods
could be transported from Newbury to London or Bristol in a mere three
hours, rather than the three days by barge. Not only was carriage by rail
very much faster, but it was not beset by long delays in times of drought or
intense cold. In the first year after the GWR reached Bristol, the Kennet
and Avon Canal receipts from lock tolls fell dramatically from some £51,000
to £41,000. In 1852 the canal was sold to the railway company and thereafter succumbed to the inevitable neglect. The fate of the Wilts and Berks
Canal was worse and by 1870 it was little more than a 'muddy trickle'.

Although the railways brought to an end the long-distance coach and
waggon trade, they stimulated the growth of local services—carriers,

105 *The* Crown Inn *and town hall at Farringdon, c.1901.*

omnibuses and cabs; which were often centred on the inns now fighting to stay profitable. The *Crown Inn* at Faringdon advertised daily coaches to and from the station; an omnibus carried commuters between Slough and Wokingham before the latter was connected with the railway. In 1854 there were more than thirty carriers operating in each of the towns of Abingdon, Newbury and Wantage, and 120 were advertised for Reading, travelling to villages all over Berkshire and places as far afield as Abingdon and High Wycombe. Wantage was also well supplied with carriers, but from 1876 it possessed what no other Berkshire town had—a tramway. Its steam-driven tram cars carried the passengers the two and half miles to connect with the Great Western railway line.

Town Development

The Victorian period witnessed a dramatic change in urban life and, by 1851, for the first time in history more people in England were living in towns than in the rural areas. This, however, was not true of Berkshire; even at the end of the century it was predominantly a rural county. Being on the railway line did not automatically bring great commercial benefits, and most Berkshire towns remained small country market towns, growing little during the second half of the century. At Hungerford the expected increase in prosperity never arrived, and its population actually declined. Only Reading developed into a busy commercial and manufacturing town, its population far out-stripping that of all the other towns. The dominant factory was that

106 *View of Reading showing the canal, railway and the town.*

of Huntley and Palmer. It had begun
as a modest biscuit, bakery and con-
fectionery shop, but the move to new
premises in 1846 enabled George
Palmer to put into operation his ideas
for the mechanisation of production.
By the 1860s it was the largest biscuit factory in England and its products were being exported to coun-
tries as far away as China and Australia. By the end of the century, with
the number of employees reaching
more than 5,000, it was the biggest
employer in the town. Reading also
boasted two other firms which became world famous—Sutton & Son,
seed merchants, and Simmond's

Brewery, both of which owed much of their success to the advantages of
railway transport.

107 *Huntley and Palmer biscuit factory from the* Illustrated London News, *1882.*

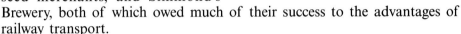

With a population of some 7,000 in 1851, New Windsor was the second largest town in the county (though a small town by national standards),
but its population was swollen by the inclusion of over a thousand soldiers
in the cavalry and infantry barracks. It had begun to grow in the early 19th
century, but the railway did not prove a stimulus to any industry except
tourism. Like several other Berkshire towns, such as Abingdon and
Wokingham, its only 'large industry' was brewing. Abingdon and Newbury
were almost the same size as New Windsor, but whereas by the end of the
century the population of New Windsor and Newbury had grown considerably, Abingdon's had scarcely grown at all. River, canal and rail contributed to the economic development of Newbury's extensive trade in corn and
malt. In the mid-19th century there were 26 corn mills within a few miles
of Newbury and, with well over two hundred traders, its corn market did
more business than Reading's. Conditions in the open market place and
rooms in the nearby inns became impossibly cramped and, after heavy rain
in 1852 caused havoc by swamping the open-air dealing, the decision was
made to build a corn exchange. The handsome, Italian-style building is still
very much a landmark at Newbury.

Of the other towns, none were bigger than large villages by today's
standards, and only Maidenhead grew substantially during the rest of the
century. Its population quadrupled from 3,603 to nearly 13,000 in 1901. Its
growth was encouraged by the railway which brought Maidenhead within
easy reach of London, but allowed it to remain a desirable place to live in
rural Berkshire. One of the townsmen who translated this into a possibility
for hundreds of newcomers was Benjamin Cail, a surveyor and designer
who put forward a plan for improving the town. Together with other local
landowners he formed the Maidenhead Improvement Company; in the 1860s

they began by buying nine acres of land near the centre of the town. By the end of the century modest villas and elegant houses lined numerous new streets north and south of the High Street, spreading eastwards to the riverside. Here the *Orkney Arms* and the *Riviera* developed into fashionable hotels with an international reputation. Maidenhead was now a fashionable resort which attracted 'excursionists', playboys and debutantes, and the cream of society, especially during Ascot Week, when Maidenhead had its own parade of boats at Boulter's Lock.

Towns like Wokingham, Wantage, Lambourn, Hungerford and Faringdon continued to serve the neighbouring parishes, providing shopping facilities and the service of a variety of small businesses and professional firms which were not available in the villages. They were also social and cultural centres, polling centres and the location of the Union workhouses. As at Wokingham there might also be the local excise office, a stamp office and savings bank, and the main post office for the area. The mail now arrived by train, not mail coach, and the introduction of postage stamps in 1840 gradually brought about an increase in the number of letters sent. In 1851 the Post Office also instituted improvements in the delivery to rural areas by the employment of messengers or foot postmen. By 1854 rural messengers at Wallingford were delivering letters to inhabitants in 19 villages; 20 villages were served by messengers from Wantage, seven from Faringdon.

Markets and fairs were still important, and the open areas of the town halls at Windsor, Abingdon, Wallingford and other towns were still used as

108 *Boulters Lock at Maidenhead early this century.*

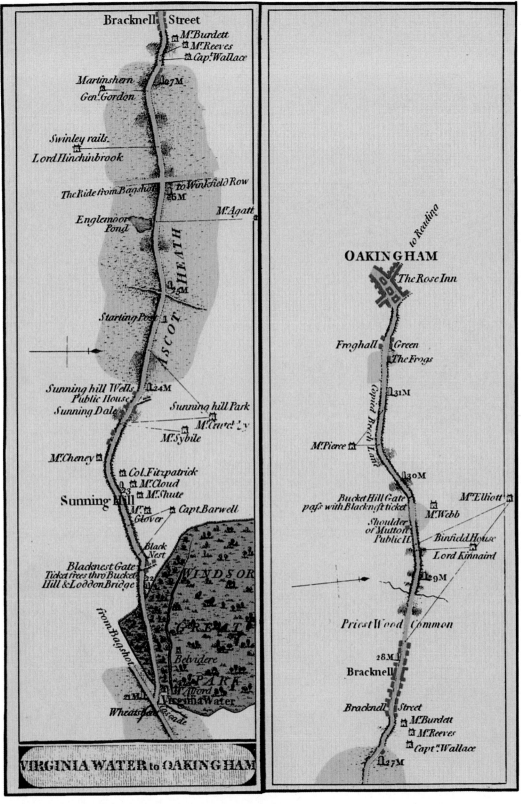

XIII *The route from Virginia Water to Oakingham as shown in John Cary's atlas of the high-roads around London, published 1 July 1790. Travel by private coach and postchaise was slow enough for travellers to appreciate the information given about the landmarks along the way.*

XIV *Windsor Castle and the River Thames.*

XV *The ancient Ridgeway near Wantage.*

109 *Farringdon cattle market.*

corn exchanges. Wokingham's weekly market was 'thinly attended' according to Billing's Directory of 1854, but, as was the case of many of Berkshire's small towns, market and fair days were the only times when they were busy. Faringdon's market, held on the first Tuesday of each month, was described as the 'monthly great market'.

The smallest of all the mid-19th-century towns was Slough. When Victoria came to the throne it was still only a village, albeit an important stage on the Bath Road. The initiative of whoever it was (probably Charles Bonsey) who persuaded the Great Western Railway Company to allow trains to stop at Slough changed that, and within a decade Slough had grown into a small market town. For 13 years it was the railway terminus for Windsor and during that time a magnificent *Royal Hotel* was built, which Queen Victoria used as a waiting room when she travelled by train. In easy reach of London, Windsor and Eton, Slough was considered a desirable place to live. There was no dominating group of developers as in Maidenhead, and most of the shops and houses were of modest size. But long before the end of the century the town had trebled in size.

In 1847 Bracknell was described in the county directory as 'a small village ... consist[ing] of a long narrow street, inhabited chiefly by shopkeepers'. It did not yet have its own church, but sometime during the second half of the century Bracknell

110 *Slough railway station and the* Royal Hotel *built by the GWR Co. c.1845. The hotel closed in 1852, only three years after the branch line to Windsor had been opened.*

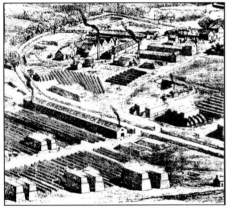

became a town. No one factor seems to have triggered this growth, but the railway came in 1856 and was important in the development of the burgeoning market gardening and brickmaking industries. A cattle and poultry market was established in 1870.

Despite the disparities of prosperity and growth, most of the towns found ways to express their civic pride. Hungerford replaced its 18th-century town hall in 1860s with a fine new building incorporating a corn exchange. At Newbury, as well as its new corn exchange, the Corporation built a new council chamber and magistrates' court; the clock tower was completed in 1881. Wantage celebrated its connection with King Alfred by erecting the magnificent marble statue of him which still dominates the Market Place. In 1887 Reading received a tremendous boost to its civic pride when first its boundaries were extended to almost double their former size, and then it was granted county borough status, confirming the independence its citizens had fought for three centuries before, but separating it from the county. This was a strange situation since it was in Reading that the offices of the newly created county council were established the following year.

111 Bracknell decorated for Queen Victoria's visit in 1845 on her way to Stratfield Saye.

112 Bracknell Pottery, Brick and Tile Co., c.1886: view of the works on either side of Folders Lane, Priestwood, Bracknell. There were brickworks also at other towns and parishes, such as Langley, Slough, Maidenhead, Twyford, Reading and Wokingham.

A plethora of authorities and boundaries

For centuries the only important boundaries to most inhabitants of Berkshire had been those of the parishes, the boroughs and the county itself. Now within a few decades a great number more were created.

The Poor Law Amendment Act of 1834 placed every parish within a Poor Union. There were 12 of these in Berkshire, the smallest being Easthampstead containing only five parishes, the largest Abingdon with 36 parishes. Each Union had its central workhouse, a symbol of the worsening attitude of the authorities to the plight of the poor. The Act set out to 'remedy the ills of the old system', in particular to cut the cost of poor relief and to improve the administration. The emphasis was on economy, and the harshness of the régime imposed in the new Union workhouses and the humiliation of wearing a drab uniform were a strong deterrent to people applying for admission until they were forced to do so. According to the Act, relief of any kind was primarily for the old and infirm, orphaned and abandoned children, and the mentally defective; no relief should be given to any able-bodied people living in their own homes. There were terrible work-houses, but it would seem that there was none of the worst kind in Berk-shire, and recent research suggests that, although harsh by today's stand-ards, they were more caring than the law advocated. The master of the Eton Union Workhouse allowed men to go out looking for work—until prevented by the Poor Law Commissioners—and elderly couples to walk together in the yard during periods of recreation. Several, like the Hungerford Union Workhouse, had schools, and all had infirmaries. Relief was also provided to people living at home and in 1840 the Unions were divided into small medical districts. There were four in Easthampstead for example—the Bracknell, Easthampstead, Sandhurst and Winkfield Districts.

The 1835 Municipal Corporations Act had created new Parliamentary boundaries which were not always coterminous with the ordinary borough boundaries. They were enlarged after a report of 1867, and in 1885 the county was divided into three Parliamentary divisions, each represented by one member. By this date only Reading and Windsor were still Parliamen-tary boroughs. In 1836 the old county was divided into 15 Registration Districts in response to two Acts passed that year which set up the system of the civil registration of births, deaths and marriages, and allowed the Superintendent Registrar to conduct purely civil marriages—a revolutionary concept for many residents. The impact of the change was quickly felt, for it enabled official statistics to be gathered, and non-conformist churches to conduct their own marriages attended only by a registrar.

Petty Session areas were now defined and from 1856, when the Berk-shire County Constabulary was formed, the county was divided into police divisions—which were not always the same as the Registration Districts or Poor Law areas. In 1900 old Berkshire had 10 police divisions, looked after by a chief constable, four inspectors, 25 sergeants and 159 constables—the day of the village bobby had arrived. No longer was law and order left in the incapable hands of the unpaid parish constable. Reading and Windsor had their own police forces which replaced the old-style watchmen who had done little more than patrol the streets at night calling out the time and weather.

From 1850 some parts of the county acquired yet another set of boun-daries with the formation of Local Boards of Health. These came about as a result of the Victorians' dawning awareness of the deleterious effects of the unsanitary conditions of the homes of the labouring population which had led to the first Public Health Act of 1848. These were urban measures, but not all towns took advantage of the Act, though according to Edwin Chadwick's report on the sanitary conditions of the labouring poor 'there was not a town in Berkshire' which would not benefit from improvements to the drainage system. Windsor and Reading were singled out for further comment. Reading Corporation had already begun to tackle the problem under a private Act of 1826. A weekly collection of household rubbish had been commenced (the first in the county) and some effort had been made to deal with the almost insurmountable problems of open cesspools, foul privies and contaminated wells, and pigsties and slaughterhouses in close proximity to dwellings and an insufficient supply of clean water. The filthy conditions of the many courts and back streets, however, were witness to the inadequate efforts of the council. Windsor, however, was the 'worst beyond all comparison', not just for the crowded insanitary conditions but for the accompanying vice.

Both Reading and New Windsor formed Local Boards of Health in 1850 and within a year had set about installing a proper drainage system, but even at the end of the century slum conditions were a disgrace in Windsor. Other towns also formed Local Health Boards, including Eton in 1850 and Slough in 1863, the areas covered in both instances being much smaller than the parishes. In the case of Eton, only the town was served although the sewage farm and infectious diseases hospital were sited in the village of Eton Wick.

Rural sanitary authorities were not formed until after the second Public Health Act of 1875. According to a royal commission the standard of cottage accommodation in Berkshire was generally poor and included examples of some of the worst in the country. Victorian paintings give a romantic view of country cottages, and today those which survive bear little resemblance to the Victorian reality summed up in the parody of a charming poem:

> The cottage homes of England
> Alas! How strong they smell
> There's fever in the cesspool
> And sewage in the well.

The end of the century brought two Acts which radically altered the structure of local government and created yet more boundaries. That of 1888 established the Berkshire County Council, an elected body which took over the administrative functions (but not the judicial) of the Quarter Sessions Court. Six years later the 1894 Civil Parishes Act removed the civil responsibilities from the parish vestries and introduced the concept of civil parishes governed by parish councils. Civil parishes were grouped in rural districts, and there were also urban districts, though old Berkshire had only one—Wantage. On the north side of the Thames (and now in Berkshire) there were also the Urban Districts of Slough and Eton. Both of these were carved out of much larger parishes, and it would seem that those who drew the new boundaries in 1894 paid as little regard to local interests as the 'draftsmen' of 1974. In both cases the remnants of the parishes were left with detached portions, an inconvenience to the residents and councillors alike.

Concern for the welfare of the community

113 *Workhouse master and paupers.*

The 19th century saw a revolution in a whole variety of matters which impinged upon the welfare of the people—rich and poor. Some were the responsibility of the statutory authorities—town councils, parish vestries and the local boards of health, but most were provided by commercial enterprises, private benevolence, churches, and charities. Each parish and town has its own story, and it is difficult to collect sufficient data to make any meaningful comparison with other counties, but some patterns and trends are clearly discernible.

Drainage schemes, street cleaning and lighting were almost always provided by the relevant statutory authority, either under one of the public health or local government Acts or a private Act of Parliament. In 1828 Wantage acquired its Improvement Act as a result of the enterprise of a number of residents, spearheaded by a local solicitor. Thirty of its most respected citizens were made commissioners responsible for the employment of watchmen, lamplighters, a surveyor, and rate collectors, rakers, cleansers, and scavengers. The provision of water and gas, on the other hand, was the work of private companies. Maidenhead, Reading and Windsor all had gas works before 1830, and gas companies were established in other towns later in the century. There was a waterworks in Reading as early as 1694, but this project was soon abandoned. A new works were established in the 18th century, but it was not until the mid-19th century that clean water, not untreated river water, began to be piped to the houses. Windsor's water supply tells a similar story, but while most of the towns had a waterworks before the end of the century, piped water did not reach many rural areas until well into this century. At first many households in towns and villages had to make-do with outside standpipes which served several houses. It was ten years after water was first brought into the village of Eton Wick in 1892 that the families in the new terraced houses in The Walk could enjoy the privilege of having a cold water tap in the kitchen; they were the first in the village.

Medical services had long been available for those who could afford to pay for them, but for the rest of the community there was scant provision and only the very poor had been the responsibility of the parish vestry. The 18th century had seen the foundation of many hospitals in the larger cities of Britain, but it was not until the next century that any were built in Berkshire. As early as 1802 a dispensary was founded in Reading through the enterprise of a group of doctors, and Windsor's dispensary was opened in 1818; they were built and maintained through donations and subscriptions, and, since there were no wards, patients were treated at the surgeries or at their homes. Medical services were provided for the poor under the Poor Law Act of 1834, but by this date there was a growing belief that there was a need for a county hospital which could treat that middling class of people

114 *Royal Berkshire Hospital, opened in 1839, the first of its kind in Berkshire.*

who could not afford to obtain private medical treatment but who did not want to be treated in the workhouse infirmaries. In 1836 work began on the hospital in London Road, Reading. William IV and Queen Adelaide became patrons and agreed that it should be called the Royal Berkshire Hospital. The opening ceremony in 1839 took place before an admiring audience of over three thousand. It was the only hospital of its kind in Berkshire.

Churches and Schools

The reform of the Church of England and expansion of the nonconformist churches had begun long before the Victorian period. Charles Wesley preached in Berkshire many times and Wesleyan societies developed at Maidenhead, Windsor, Newbury and several other centres. By the beginning of Victoria's reign the Methodist Church was not only firmly established, but had divided into several branches, notably the Wesleyans, the Primitive Methodists and the Countess of Huntingdon's Connexion. Villages and towns were 'missioned' and meetings were held in the open air, cottages and barns until money was raised for purpose-built chapels. A similar story of missioning can be told of the Congregational and Baptists Churches, and nonconformist churches and chapels were not infrequently the first ecclesiastical buildings to be built in a village which did not contain an ancient parish church. Bracknell, Chalvey, Brimpton, and Woodley are examples from different parts of the county.

New churches and the creation of new parishes were a physical expression of the changes occurring within the established church which can be found in every part of the county. The churches at Bradfield, Shaw-cum-Donnington and Burghfield are just three examples of parishes churches rebuilt in the 19th century. St Sebastian's at Wokingham and St Peter's at Earley, on the other hand, were new churches which soon became the centre of newly created parishes in the suburbs of Wokingham and Reading respectively. St John the Baptist's at Eton Wick was a daughter chapel serving the rapidly growing village; it replaced the schoolroom which had been used for church services for some twenty years.

115 *The new parish church at Burghfield.*

The Victorians were horrified at the paucity of church attendance revealed by the one and only ecclesiastical census which was taken in 1851, but parish magazines also reveal a picture of churches with full congregations and Sunday Schools and programmes of church work which touched almost every aspect of the lives of the parishioners. New charities were set up and money was found for such things as maternity boxes for poor mothers, provident societies, reading rooms, savings banks, and the provision of tickets which could be used to get medical services at the nearby dispensary. Church and chapel ministers universally now had a pastoral rôle, a situation which had been not been prevalent at the beginning of the century.

Education was also very much a church affair. The survey of schools conducted by the government in 1833 revealed a very mixed picture, with some villages such as Catmere without a school of any kind, and others with schooling being provided by charitable parishioners, the local church, and private enterprise.

BRIMPTON Parish (Pop. 443)—One Sunday School (commenced 1829), containing 18 males and 20 females; supported by voluntary contributions.

BRIGHTWALTHAM Parish (Pop. 442)—One daily school, wherein 12 males and 18 females are educated and clothed at the sole expense of the rector.

BUCKLAND with CARSWELL Parish (Pop. 946)—Two daily schools, one of which is endowed and contains 30 females, in the other from 30 to 50 males are under instruction at the expense of their parents; the above schools are also opened for the benefit of the parish on Sundays, and about 30 males and 40 females receive gratuitous instruction.

That year, 1833, saw the beginning of the government's interest in education with the passing of an Act of Parliament authorising grants to schools. It was the first of many Education Acts and only one of many forces of change which encouraged the provision of schooling for every child. By 1851, when an educational census was taken, Berkshire had 610 schools, of which 346 were private. There were also 306 Sunday Schools and 13 evening schools for adults. The great majority of the schools provided only an elementary education—fitting the pupils, as so many of those in authority believed, for their lowly status as labourers or servants. But Berkshire also had its share of old established grammar schools such as Eton College, Reading and Abingdon grammar schools, which were said to have been founded in the Middle Ages, and Saint Bartholomew's Grammar School at Newbury. There were also a few new ones including Bradfield College, one of the earliest endowed grammar schools of the Victorian era, Wellington College, founded in 1859 for the orphan sons of army officers, and Salt Hill Grammar School,

116 *Village school at Stanford in the Vale.*

a private school which flourished for some three decades and offered an education to the sons of tradesmen. In 1885 Oxford University began a series of lectures in Reading—a small beginning, but an important one in the story of the University Extension Movement. It led to the establishment of Reading College in 1892 and the University of Reading in 1926.

The variety of schools available in the larger towns reflects something of the character and attitudes of their townsfolk. For example, at Windsor it was the churches (established and nonconformist) which were the driving force, not the Corporation and, on the eve of the great Education Act of 1870 in just one part of the town, St Stephen's parish, there was a mission (or ragged) school, an infants school, a boys school, and a girls middle school (for the daughters of tradesmen), all founded by the nuns of the House of Mercy, an Anglican nunnery which itself had been founded in 1851 to rescue 'fallen women'. Before the end of the century the nuns also opened St Stephen's High School and a college for the daughters of clergymen. At Old Windsor there were industrial schools which taught laundry work and cooking to the girls and gardening to the boys.

Golden years and deep depression

Throughout the 19th century more people in Berkshire were working on the land than were employed in any other occupation, except perhaps domestic service. By 1837, when Victoria came to the throne, many of the difficulties hampering the increased use of scientific methods of farming had been removed, and many landowners and farmers, though few farm labourers, were benefiting from the changes. Corn laws passed in 1815, however, protected English agriculture, and there was a growing movement in the country for free trade and the abolition of these laws. An anti-corn law league was founded in 1838 which four years later extended its organisation by establishing 12 regional centres, the southern district covering the counties of Gloucestershire, Wiltshire, Hampshire and Berkshire. Local farmers and landowners responded to the threat and at a meeting held in the *Upper Ship Inn*, Reading, under the chairmanship of Col. Blagrave of Calcot Park, they formed the Berkshire Association for the Protection of Agriculture. Committee members came from all parts of the county, including Reading, Wallingford, Sonning, Twyford, Newbury, Lambourn, Blewbury and the Wantage area. The president was W. Mount of Wasing Place.

117 *Royal Agricultural Society Meeting at Windsor, 1851.*

The conflict between the two societies and the agitation against the corn laws brought to light numerous unfair practices working against the tenant farmers and the belief of the Berkshire protectionists that labourers' wages should be kept as low as possible. The speeches of the Members of Parliament representing Berkshire (reported at length in the local newspapers) were directed at the farming element in the population and those in the trades that depended on agriculture. In 1846 all three members cast their vote against the repeal of the corn laws, but they were on the losing side.

Although many, possibly the majority, of Berkshire farmers believed that the loss of protection was

a betrayal, agriculture did not immediately suffer and the years 1846 to the 1870s were an exceedingly prosperous period with people being willing to put money into farming. The railway made the London market increasingly accessible to Berkshire farmers, and the early morning collection of milk for London became a familiar sight in many parts of the county. In 1865 the Great Western Railway was carry 9,000 gallons of milk to London daily, but that year a cattle plague virtually wiped out the London cowkeepers, and the following year the railway transported 144,000 gallons. Queen Victoria was patron of the newly formed Royal Agricultural Society of England which held a magnificent show in the Home Park at Windsor in 1851. Prince Albert and the Prince of Wales both served as president at different times, and under instructions from Prince Albert extensive work was carried out on the royal farms. One of the most splendid dairies in the country was built at Frogmore in the Home Park at Windsor. There were others of importance on Col. Loyd-Lindsay's estate at Ardington and of lesser importance at Bloomfield Hatch Farm at Grazeley.

By 1880 the golden years of agriculture were over. Three years of bleak springs and rainy summers spelt disaster for arable and livestock farming, and the country suffered from economic depressions and periods of inflation for much of the last quarter of the 19th century. The fears of the protectionists materialised with the importation of cheap corn from Canada and wool and lamb from New Zealand and Australia; the first cargo of frozen lamb reached London in 1882. The production of cheese and butter in Berkshire was only of small importance, but the import and marketing of these products through Danish dairy co-operatives put Berkshire farmers, who were mainly selling to local shops, at a great disadvantage, and much of the farmhouse cheese which was sold at the Reading Michaelmas cheese fair was sold at a loss.

Prices of other products, particularly wool, fell disastrously. The great sheep farming area in Berkshire was still the Berkshire Downs. Upland fields which had been ploughed up during the good years for feeding the sheep on root crops were allowed to tumble to grass. Water meadows were abandoned and the sheep population decreased dramatically. Farms failed and soon land agents were reporting that tenants could not be found for the vacant farms. Arable farmers suffered just as badly as the price of corn plummetted. Those farmers who survived were often the ones who had adopted new methods of farming, such as dairying, reduced their labour force, and perhaps invested in new machinery.

Amongst those who did so in Berkshire were John Walter of Bearwood Farm, near Wokingham and George Baylis of Wyfield Manor near Newbury. It was the beginning of a new pattern of agriculture in Berkshire. John Walter, owner of *The Times*, could afford to put money into his farming interests and in the 1880s he bought a steam plough, the first in use in Berkshire. George Baylis introduced a cropping system on his newly purchased 400-acre farm which did not rely on animal manure for maintaining soil fertility. Instead he used artificial fertilisers and new varieties of corn.

118 *Ploughing team.*

Believing that by enlarging the area farmed he could substantially reduce his overheads, Baylis took the opportunity to lease other farms that came on to the market at very favourable terms of tenancy. By the end of the century he was farming more than 4,000 acres and by 1917 he was the largest arable farmer in England with over 12,000 acres in Berkshire and Hampshire. But it was not just the size of his holdings that were large; so were his fields after the removal of many miles of hedgerows. His workforce, on the other hand, numbered only about two hundred. He was a key figure in the transition to modern concepts of agriculture.

The Shopping revolution

Until the early 19th century few villages in Berkshire, or elsewhere in the country, contained a shop where groceries or household goods could be purchased. What could not be provided by the villagers themselves must be sought in the neighbouring town or from an itinerant hawker or cheap jack. By the beginning of Victoria's reign, however, village shops—usually grocers, general dealers, bakers or butchers—were to be found everywhere in the county. Few villages did not have at least one. Not many goods on sale were of the ready-prepared variety or even packaged—that was done by the shopkeeper while the customer waited and watched—but most village shops stocked a very large variety of goods. The ledgers of Edward Allnutt of Sonning, grocer and baker in the 1860s, list bread and cakes, flour, yeast, oatmeal, currants, tea, coffee, bacon, pork, fruit, sweets, starch, matches, blacklead, bird seed and coal. As the 19th century progressed, a new range

119 *Village shop at Brimpton: supply stores, baker and grocer.*

of processed groceries became available, sold at prices that all but the
poorest could afford. The cottager
had at last joined the consumer society. Amongst these packaged and
processed goods were biscuits made
by Huntley and Palmer of Reading,
lemonade by Mainwood's of Windsor, Elliman's embrocation made at
Slough, and a fish sauce made by
Cocks of Reading.

One-man or family businesses
predominated, but there were a few
run by co-operative societies. These
were usually found in villages or
towns with strong associations with
industry. The Slough Co-op was
founded in the 1890s to combat the
hardship being suffered by families during a strike by local brickmakers.
Ardington Co-op Store, on the other hand, was the result of the philan-
thropic endeavours of Lord Wantage who wanted to encourage thrift in the
villagers.

120 *Sports department of Herbert's department store, Eton.*

Itinerant salesmen still visited the villages, a few still on foot, but there
was a growing number of town shops offering a service to the villages, and
general carriers which acted as shopping agents, taking orders from village
people for individual items as diverse as reels of cotton or a garden spade.
In the towns the number of shops and small businesses had mushroomed.
Reading had more than 1,600 according to Billing's directory of 1854,
Newbury and Windsor more than 500 each. Lambourn, one of the smallest
of Berkshire's towns, had at least 140 and Slough, which had only been a
town for some twelve years, already had a High Street and was beginning
to challenge the older South Buckinghamshire town of Eton.

One other retail outlet which was very much a feature of the Victorian
village was the public house or beer shop; the latter was not strictly a shop,
but a public house which could only sell beer (not spirits or wine) either on
or off the premises according to the licence. They had come into existence
as a result of the Beer Act of 1830 which, as its preamble states, was for the
better supply of beer. The government was concerned about the recent increase in the consumption of gin following a lowering of the excise duties
on spirits. The Act did not achieve its aim of reducing the amount of spirits
drunk, but it was certainly successful in making beer more available. Hundreds of beer shops were opened in Berkshire, some of them in villages, such
as Purley and Cippenham, which had been without a public house since
licensing became more effective a hundred years or so years earlier. The
beer shops were often little more than an ordinary cottage or terrace house
whose owner purchased a barrel of beer from the nearest brewery and set

121 George and Dragon *beer shop at Swallowfield.*

122 *Simmond's Brewery of Reading.*

it up in the kitchen. Many of them were free houses, but Simmond's Brewery of Reading bought more than forty properties in anticipation of the Act and opened them as beer shops as soon as the Act was passed.

In 1887 and 1897 villagers and townsfolk all over the country celebrated the Golden and Diamond Jubilees commemorating the 50 and 60
years that Victoria had been queen. Contemporary comment dwelt on the
achievements which had made Britain a great country, the decorations and
prodigious feasts that were provided in way of celebration. In reality they
had not been 'Sixty Glorious Years' for many people in Berkshire, but the
village of 1897, with its church and chapel, village shop, school, policeman,
and a workingmen's club or village hall, was very different from that of 60
years earlier.

123 *The Wilts and Berks canal near Wantage.*

7

The Age of the Motor, 1895 onwards

124 *A* Punch *cartoon depicting a police speed trap. The early years of motoring were characterised by the hostile attitude of the police and magistrates.*

On 3 July 1895 the Hon Evelyn Ellis of Datchet made the first car journey on an English road in his newly purchased Panhard automobile. It was something of a test case—was this new four-wheeled petrol vapour conveyance a carriage or a locomotive? There were restrictive laws about the use of both. In the event the journey was uneventful, and within a short time Ellis' personal campaign to show the unfrightening aspect of motor vehicles had been reinforced by newly formed associations of enthusiasts. Much of the rest of the story of the early growth of motor transport is national history rather than special to Berkshire, though the Hon Evelyn Ellis continued to play an important part in it, and at Rosenau, his home in Datchet, he demonstrated the power of the combustion engine by temporarily converting his motor car into a fire engine. He also gave Edward, Prince of Wales, his first drive in 1896.

Royal patronage for motoring did much to help the automobile lobby. That same year the Locomotive Emancipation Act opened up the use of the roads to motor traffic, albeit restricted to a maximum speed of 12 mph— but that was a great improvement on four mph previously in force. Motoring quickly grew in popularity, soon becoming a sport for those who could afford to import a car and enjoy the pleasures of driving, rallying and racing. During the Automobile Club's Easter Tour of 1899 Charles Jarrott ran his Panhard into a sheep in the dark, on the outskirts of Reading. But already the opposition was growing, and many of the county police forces and magistrates were openly and actively hostile. In July 1899 *The Autocar* published a report of how a Mr Lyons Sampson had been waylaid at Colnbrook in what was described as a 'police trap' and charged before the Slough magistrates for having failed to stop his motor car when called upon to do so by a man (a police constable out of uniform) in charge of a horse and cart. This conflict between authorities and motorists lasted more than two decades and was no worse in Berkshire than many other counties, but

125 *Berkshire Automobile Club badge.*

the map published in a 1903 issue of *The Autocar* pinpointing the principal police trap locations showed three in Berkshire on the Bath Road between Hare Hatch and Hungerford.

Despite the opposition and the legal restrictions the motor car was here to stay, and by the early years of the 20th century it was making an impact quite as impressive as the railway had done 70 years earlier. Garages selling petrol and tyres were to be found in the towns, and AA motor scouts were seen patrolling the Bath Road as far west as Twyford. In 1904 the speed limit was raised to 20 mph and individual towns and villages, such as Slough, Colnbrook, and Reading, successfully petitioned for a mere 10 mph through the built-up area. Other local councils, such as Eton Wick, complained about the dust nuisance but could do little about it—except use a water-cart to dampen the road. At Twyford the dust and general dreadful state of the roads gave rise to an acrimonious dispute through letters to the *Reading Mercury*, which eventually persuaded the parish council to tar the roads at a cost of some £40, a sum which was mainly raised through subscriptions. Cyclists and motorists also began to put pressure on the government to improve the roads. In 1913 an International Road Conference was held at Reading and stretches of the Bath Road at Twyford were surfaced with a variety of materials as demonstration of their differences. By the end of that year the whole length of the Bath Road through Berkshire had been resurfaced—the first in the county to be tarmacadamed.

The years immediately before the first world war saw a notable expansion of practical services by cycling and motoring organisations, such as town and village signs, road signs and AA boxes, and lists of recommended hotels. The *Bear* at Hungerford, the *Shillingford Bridge* at Wallingford, the *Swan* at Streatley, and the *Bear* at Wantage were in the first AA list of 1909.

126 *AA hotel sign.*

127 *Advertisement from* Kelly's Directory *of 1915.*

These years also saw the beginning of a motor and cycle manufacturing industry in Berkshire, albeit quite small. Kelly's directories of Berkshire for 1903 and Buckinghamshire for 1907 advertise 33 cycle manufacturers in old and new Berkshire, and by 1915 there were three motor car manufacturers, as well as 34 motor engineers, motor agents, motor accessory manufacturers, repairers, and body builders, as well as 17 garages. Most of these were in the main towns, but Cookham Rise enterprises featured in three lists.

Berkshire's (or more accurately, Buckinghamshire's) connection with motoring took an interesting turn when in 1917 the War Office

Motor Deliveries

are now the vogue with every up-to-date Business House.

The Best Car for light loads, up to 6 cwt. in either Town or Country is a

WARRICK MOTOR CARRIER

As successfully employed by many of the leading Houses throughout London and the Provinces.

All particulars from the Sole Manufacturers:

John Warrick & Co., Ltd.,

Caversham Road, READING.

——o——

Prices, complete with lettering, all Accessories and Tools, **from 100 Guineas.**

established a Mechanical Transport Repair Depot on land to the west of Slough, in the cornfields of Cippenham Court Farm. The Depot should have been capable of repairing 100 lorries, 100 cars and 130 motor cycles per week. But what was intended as a 'hospital for crippled motor transport' soon looked more like a motoring graveyard and local people nicknamed it the Dump. Work commenced, but when hostilities ended the Depot was still under construction and there were more than a thousand war vehicles in need of repair. To the government the site had

128 *Broken cars, motor cycles and lorries at the War Office Motor Vehicle Depot at Cippenham, near Slough, c.1919.*

become a financial embarrassment and they were relieved when in 1920 a group of business men offered to buy the Depot and all the vehicles, at home and abroad. The Slough Trading Estate was born. It was a bold venture, but by the end of the year the plant had been made operational and the Company had sold war office surplus vehicles to the value of £5 million. Their auctions were widely advertised and people came from all over the country, anxious to buy cars, lorries, motor cycles and ambulances. No doubt some were bought by the motor transport firms which were being established in Berkshire towns. The Thatcham Road Transport Services in Chapel Street and G L Barkham's haulage and removal service at Thatcham were both founded in 1919.

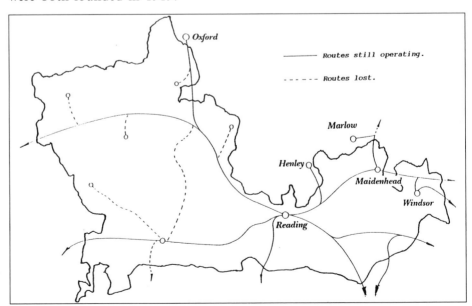

129 *Berkshire's depleted railway network, c.1960.*

In the 1920s Twyford and Colnbrook became two of the first places in the county to be by-passed, measures which were aimed at relieving the residents from the nuisance of the motor car and to provide work for de-mobbed soldiers. Waterer's Nursery objected to the construction of the Twyford bypass fearing that it would adversely affect their business, but after its completion the firm erected a sign announcing 'Waterer's Floral Mile'—a name which is still remembered with pleasure. By the 1950s the problems of traffic congestion had become acute. Towns on the Bath Road which had originally prospered from their position on a main trade route now found that the value of the passing trade had diminished to a point when it was far less important than the inconvenience it caused. Already there was talk of a London-South Wales Motor-Way. Work began on the M4 in the mid-1960s, though the middle section through Berkshire and Wiltshire was not completed until 1971. Traffic counts the previous year along the A4 showed some 30,000 cars travelling daily between Reading and Maidenhead Thicket when the capacity was only 13,000 cars. Traffic along the Newbury to Hungerford section dropped from 8,000 vehicles a day to 3,000 after the motorway opened. At Theale the traffic dropped almost to nil, for the village was by-passed, and is today a pleasant backwater.

Motorway, dual carriageways, by-passes, lay-bys, roundabouts, cats eyes, traffic signs, bollards, contraflow systems, ring roads—the changes and additions to our roads continue. In this Berkshire is no different from any other county, but the impact of the motor vehicle is woven into almost every aspect of its 20th-century history.

Suburban county—estates and neighbourhoods

Berkshire is no longer a rural county for, although it is still possible to drive or walk for miles along country lanes or highways passing through farming areas, only a small proportion of its inhabitants are connected with the land. Villages are mostly suburban in character even in predominantly farming areas, such as the Vale of the White Horse. But, whereas in the past the drift of people from working on the land had almost inevitably meant rural depopulation, the development of a motor car-owning population has allowed people to live in country villages and town suburbs while working several miles away. Even Hungerford in the far west of the county is within com-muting distance of London. The steady growth of population seen in the 19th century continued during the first half of this century, but thereafter it quickened considerably. It almost doubled between 1951 and 1991, show-ing Berkshire to have one of the fastest growing populations in the country.

This aspect of the county's history might be said to begin soon after the Great War with the passing of the Act of Parliament which brought into being the first council houses. They were conceived as 'homes for heroes', and in many a parish and town the first tenants were ex-soldiers. The numbers of houses built at this date were relatively small, but as the century

130 *Council houses at Aldermaston. The first council houses were built soon after the First World War—homes for soldiers and their families.*

131 *The main entrance to Slough Trading Estate during the 1930s. For some years the estate was almost a self-contained unit with its own gates, post office, banks, railway station, power station, fire station and ambulance.*

progressed council estates became larger and a very distinctive feature of town and country.

Town expansion has been greatest in the south of the county, where suburbs spread over farmland and encompassed neighbouring villages and hamlets. Reading extended far beyond its ancient boundaries absorbing the parishes of Caversham, Earley, Woodley and Tilehurst, although not all of these are within its modern District boundaries. In the 1980s Lower Earley housing estate, with a population of over 10,000, was the fastest growing estate in Western Europe.

In the 1920s Slough was still a small country town, but the success of the new trading estate was already having its effect. While most of the country suffered badly during the years of the Depression, Slough had one of the lowest unemployment figures in the country. Its early operation of repairing and selling cars was over by 1924 and the firm then changed its name to Slough Estates Ltd and became the first of its kind—an industrial estate providing factory premises which it leased to manufacturers together with the necessary services. By 1930 the Estate had more than a hundred tenants employing some 8,000 workers, many of whom had moved to Slough from the depressed areas of South Wales and the North. The *Daily Mail* described Slough as the 'hardest working town in Britain' where overtime not short-time was the order of the day and factories could not be built fast enough to absorb all the potential labour. New housing could not keep up with the demand though more than 4,000 private and council houses were built during the 1920s and 1930s, most of them in the neighbouring parishes. In 1930 the urban district boundaries were extended to take in parts of the parishes of Burnham, Farnham Royal, Stoke Poges, Wexham and Langley Marish. In 1938 the town was designated a borough. By then it had a population of over 50,000, a far cry from that of a hundred years earlier.

The growth of Bracknell was very different, for it was one of the eight New Towns built soon after World War II to provide both houses and industries to replace those destroyed in London by air raids. Under the Greater London Plan a Green Belt area was established to prevent further expansion of the built-up area; beyond this were the

'overspill towns'. The original plan had recommended White Waltham as the site of a new town, but the high quality of the agricultural land and the proximity of Waltham airfield ruled this out, and eventually in June 1949 an official order designated an area of 1,860 acres (753 hectares) on the infertile sandy soils further south to become the site of Bracknell New Town.

These new towns were planned as self-contained country towns where the residents could find homes, work, facilities for shopping, schools, and social and cultural activities—not merely dormitory suburbs, nor industrial estates. Such high-flown ideals did not meet with universal approval; indeed there was plenty of opposition, much of it from Berkshire people who found they could not be accommodated in the new houses. As a New Town it was expected to draw its population and industry mainly from linked areas of western Middlesex or the county of London, and many firms came from such places as Paddington, Battersea, Brixton, Brentford, Ealing and Heston.

132 *Point Royal Tower, Bracknell.*

Under the aegis of the Development Corporation, Bracknell grew rapidly. The first factory was in production by 1952, and by 1961 the population had quadrupled. Three of the nine neighbourhoods—Priestwood, Easthampstead and Bulbrook—were well on the way to completion, each eventually with its own centre and facilities. Landscaping was a very important and successful feature of the town plan, but in one respect at least the original plan failed badly. This was in the provision of garages, the Ministry ruling that 21 garages for every 100 houses was quite sufficient!

It was a miscalculation that affected new residential areas all over the county. The new concept of neighbourhood town planning was also used in other towns and, like the centre of Bracknell, most other Berkshire towns have been redeveloped, losing in the process many of their old established shops and public houses. Branches of national retail outlets have opened in every High Street, and on the outskirts supermarkets and DIY stores are found in profusion.

The patterns of industry have also changed. The Vale of the White Horse is notable for its concentration of scientific establishments, such as the Atomic Energy Research Establishment near Harwell (now trading as AEA Technology) and the Rutherford/Appleton Laboratory at Chilton. Several new industrial estates and business parks have been built in recent years, most of them adjacent to major highways, particularly the A4, A34 and A329(M). Distant views of the cooling towers at Didcot and Slough, and the distinctive lines of Courage's Brewery as one passes by it on the M4, are constant reminders of Berkshire's industrial rôle, but for the most part the nature of its industrial and commercial activities are hidden away inside anonymous buildings. Few people would describe Berkshire as an industrial county, a phrase which evokes a picture of heavy engineering works, but in recent years the term 'Silicon Valley' has been used to describe the concentration of light industry based on the micro-chip in the Thames Valley, and now Berkshire is at the heart of the Golden Triangle, an area of prime business sites stretching from the M40 to the M3 and westwards to Newbury.

There are still small rural communities, some of which have become more isolated with the loss of post office, village school and bus service. Occasionally such villages, like the Wiltshire village of Snap which lies only a few miles west of the county boundary, have become completely depopulated; its last family abandoned its home in the 1930s. More fortunate, perhaps, are those which become a 'commuter oasis', depopulated only during the day when adults are away at work and the children at school. This could have happened to the villages of Lockinge and Ardington on the Lockinge Estate, for by 1950 the mechanisation of farming had drastically reduced the number of estate workers needed. Early in the 1970s, however, Christopher Loyd, the estate owner, and his agent put into operation a practical scheme to save the two villages. Redundant farm buildings were converted for small businesses and crafts workshops, providing jobs for more than a hundred residents. A village trust renovated old cottages and built new homes, including ones for old people and young couples, and a local enterprise scheme now links Lockinge and Ardington with three other neighbouring villages. Harvests, haymaking and shearing are no longer major events in the year in these villages, but they are very much communities. So are many other places, despite the criticism that people do not care as they did in the 'old days'. Such community spirit does not always exist—perhaps it never did—but in towns, villages and suburbs there are plenty of communal activities as a glance at any parish magazine will show. The need to put down roots and to have a feeling of belonging is very real and perhaps explains the growing number of local history societies in the county and local history publications.

Farming—change and more change
The first three decades of the 20th century saw a continuation of the pattern of decline begun in the late 1870s, as the comparison of the acreage under cereals and the number of sheep clearly shows:

	1872	1922	1972
Crops		**Acreages**	
Cereals	149,486	97, 215	155,062
Permanent grasses	111,857	161,732	72,260
Livestock		**Nos. of animals**	
Cattle	31,919	53,428	95,591
Sheep	271,881	67,617	51,332
Pigs	47,438	20,372	126,132
Horses used for agriculture	13,920	8,708	-

133 *Driving sheep to East Ilsley Fair, c.1930.*

There were still numerous vacant farms prior to 1914—Burghfield Place Farm and Knights Farm to name but two—and there were others like Alden Farm at Upton near Didcot where in the 1920s the farmer struggled to make a subsistence living. On large areas of the downs sheep were allowed to graze at will without the care of a shepherd. Sometimes the landowner would try to take over the farm himself, but this often resulted in even greater losses, and good landlords, such as Squire Godsal of Haines Hill Estate at Twyford, found it better to waive rents in order to tide good tenants over the bad years. The folding system of combining sheep and corn farming was no longer viable; instead more prolific breeds of sheep were brought in from Mid-Wales and the Borders of Scotland which did well on grass pasture, needing far less labour. Loyd of Lockinge, the biggest land-owner in Berkshire at this period, brought in some 3,000 Welsh ewes for his farms. But sheep farming was never again to be of great importance in Berkshire and in 1934 the East Ilsley fair was held for the last time.

The number of farm workers declined dramatically and tragically, from some 18,000 labourers and 841 shepherds in 1891 to 6,500 and 524 respectively in 1911, and numbers have continued to decline ever since. Against this depressing picture of farming in Berkshire there was, however, a new and hopeful element—the arrival of hard-working, determined farmers from Cumbria and Scotland to whom Berkshire, despite the economic difficulties, offered much better prospects than those of their homelands. Good land-owners, such as the Benyons of Englefield and the Loyds of Lockinge, welcomed such tenants. Dairy farming, already an important industry, in-creased its production, and by 1911 a quarter of all the milk sent to London

134 *Milk churns: the one on the left with the muslin cover (weighted at the edges with blue beads) is cooling after milking.*

135 *An early machine for spraying weed killer based on sulphuric acid produced at the Jealott's Hill research establishment.*

came from Berkshire and Wiltshire. In 1900 there were a mere five churns waiting daily at Kintbury railway station, the product of just one farm. By 1911, 15 farmers were producing enough milk to fill 46 churns each day. The old system of milk prices had been superseded by an agreement with London wholesale milk buyers, such as the Model Dairies at Ealing and the Great Western Dairies at Paddington, and the fortnightly milk cheque became a vital part of the farmers' income. Farming was also becoming more scientific. James Steel of Manor Farm, Grazeley co-operated with the nearby National Institute for Research in Dairying. He was in the forefront of agricultural improvement, practising the most up-to-date methods of clean milk production at a time when TB was still the scourge of the dairy industry. He also used fertilisers on his pasture and mechanised his milking and arable cropping.

By the First World War a few farms, such as Mile House Farm at Theale or Dickie Froud's at Childrey, had invested in a tractor, but for

136 *Harvesting on the Berkshire Downs with a Massey-Harris combine harvester in the 1950s. Notice the haystacks in the distance.*

137 *Haymaking on the Lockinge Estate, a labour intensive job in 1905.*

most Berkshire farmers this was not a financial or practical possibility. There were only 11 tractors on the Lockinge Estate of some 4,000 acres in 1935 and in 1940 there were still 4,600 heavy horses used on the land in Berkshire. But it was American and British tractors that were responsible for converting 20,000 acres of permanent pasture into tillage as part of the war effort to feed the country. By the 1950s tractors had replaced horses on all but a few farms. Instead of a pair of horses pulling a single plough to till only three quarters of an acre of wet clay on Manor Farm at Grazeley, Bill Biggar who took over from James Steel could plough 30 acres in a day using a large horse-power tractor with four-furrow reversible plough. Further mechanisation brought such labour-saving devices as combine harvesters and milking parlours, and when Bill Biggar retired in 1983 there was only one farm employee as against the six employed by James Steel in the 1930s.

Gone now are the haystacks and the fields full of sheaves of corn arranged in stooks, and the sight of almost the whole of a village community helping with hay making. Gone too is the back-breaking work of weeding fields by hand, and no longer do we see fields red with poppies or yellow with charlock, though new crops such as oilseed rape and linseed add their splash of colour. Gone too from most of the farms is the familiar sight of a herd of Dairy Shorthorns, replaced perhaps by Ayrshires, but milk quotas and other forces have reduced the dairy herds, and in Grazeley and elsewhere there are now none at all. There are still plenty of horses in Berkshire, but they are found in riding stables, at the race course at Ascot, Windsor and Newbury or training on the Berkshire downs. at Lambourn and the

138 *Manure ready for spreading on Manor Farm at Grazeley in the 1930s—a lonely back-breaking job.*

Letcombes, and reckoned as part of the leisure industry or racing world—not agriculture.

Rolls of Honour

Every village has its war memorial recording the names of those who died in the two great wars, and the sale of poppies and Armistice Day services are annual reminders of world events which struck at the lives of people in every part of Berkshire. Recent anniversaries of D Day and VE Day have brought memories of the last war to the fore, revealing details long forgotten and not always recorded.

Perhaps the greatest upheaval to many places occurred in the early months of the war with the evacuation of children and refugees from London. Berkshire was far enough away from the capital to be considered a safe county, and in Reading alone 9,000 householders received billeting notices. Some 25,000 children arrived at Reading in the first week of September—but official organisation was not well co-ordinated and they were four days late. Altogether Berkshire took 46,722 evacuees, almost double the number expected. For some children and host families evacuation was a happy experience despite the crowding and shortages. So many people moved into Reading that in 1941 it was designated a 'closed town'. Purley-on Thames became a reception area for two distinct groups of people—official evacuees and owners of riverside holiday homes and plots of land who moved to Purley for the duration of the war.

139 *Ruscombe war memorial.*

140 *Evacuees arriving at Reading.*

Few bombs fell on Berkshire, but in 1943 a string of bombs fell on Reading killing 41 people and injuring many more. That same year a hit-and-run raid by a single Dornier plane demolished St John's Church at Newbury and several other buildings and killed 15 people. A thick pall of oily black smokescreen camouflaged Slough Trading Estate where many of the factories had been requisitioned for war work, including the manufacture of incendiary bombs and Spitfires. Hurricanes, designed by Sydney Camm of Windsor, were built at the Hawker aircraft factory at Langley. The Phillips and Powis aircraft factory at Woodley designed new types of trainer aircraft for the RAF—the Miles Magister and the Miles Master. At Tubney Wood, Bofor anti-aircraft guns were manufactured in a secret factory in a dense pinewood near the Oxfordshire border; there was a Bofor Ack Ack tower on the Brocas at Eton. Part of Greenham Common was occupied by the 101 US Division and from here planes took off to take part in the invasion of Europe on D-Day 1944. After the war the Air Ministry acquired most of Greenham and Crookham Commons for conversion into a heavy bomber base for the American Air Force. In 1981 the base began to be used as a USAF Cruise Missile base, and the protests by people, many of them women, against nuclear weapons brought Greenham into the national news for several years.

Air-raid sirens and Anderson shelters, doodle bugs, dog fights and barrage balloons, civil defence, home guard units and ARP regulations, land girls, rationing and recipes with unusual ingredients—memories of these are common to almost everyone who lived through World War II in Berkshire

141 *Miles Master aeroplane.*

or elsewhere in the country. In the summer of 1940 the appearance of many places changed as the government order to collect iron railings for scrap was carried out. Unfortunately much of this scrap was never used and some of it was left in a siding at Reading Station for many years. A 'Digging for Victory' campaign was taken up everywhere, not least in Windsor where part of the Great Park was converted to arable farmland. Towns raised huge sums of money to pay for warships during War Weapons Week in 1941. Pill boxes were built alongside the Kennet and Avon Canal and there were prisoner of war camps at Mortimer and Maidenhead. For a short period in 1939 Billingsgate fish market was moved to Datchet, and early in the war Caversham Park became the home of the BBC's Monitoring Service which played a vital rôle in disseminating information. It was here that the first news was received of the capitulation of Germany in May 1945.

'Here to serve'

The latter years of the 19th century saw the introduction of new structures in the government of Berkshire—the formation of the first Berkshire County Council in 1888/9 and the civil parishes and urban districts in 1894/5. At both county and local level there were boundary changes—Dedworth, formerly a detached area of the parish of New Windsor, became part of Clewer parish; Sunninghill parish was created out of Old Windsor. No attempt was made, however, to unite the old village of Eton Wick with New Town just across the parish boundary, although Eton Wick was made a parish in its own right and New Town was more than a mile from its parish centre at Boveney. Colnbrook remained divided between parishes and counties.

The creation of civil parishes brought an end to the old system of parish vestries. In future church affairs would be in the hands of parochial church councils and the civil government of the parishes would be the responsibility of the newly elected parish or urban district councils. All ratepayers had the right to vote and the first meetings of the newly elected councils were held in December 1894 or early in 1895. A perusal of the names of these first councillors and their chairmen suggests that, as one might expect, some places, like Childrey, Eton Wick and Lockinge, remained dominated by a local family or institution. Major Dunn served as chairman of Childrey Parish Council from 1894 to 1926; Edward Vaughan, Eton College Master, became the first chairman of the Eton Wick Parish Council, and retained the post for over twenty years.

Much of the work of the parish councils was concerned with the upkeep of footpaths and footbridges, but they also acted as watchdogs, requesting, negotiating with and chivvying the rural district councils and other authorities to do their jobs properly—cleaning the ditches and village ponds, dealing with cesspits, and preventing the mis-use of the commons. The parish rate, however, was very small and most councils were hampered by a lack of funds. Childrey tried to get street lighting in 1896 and 1936, but failed because of the expense. Eton Wick formally decided not to adopt the Lighting Act of 1895, nor to order the payment of an extra hospital rate to

Eton Urban District Council so that its parishioners could attend the Eton cottage hospital and, each time the questions of main drainage and schemes for refuse collection were brought up, discussions were terminated because of the 'prohibitive cost'. In some matters, however, most councils no doubt made positive contributions to the quality of village life. For example, Twyford council bought seven acres of land in 1913 for use as allotments. Bucklebury organised the parish celebrations for the coronation of Edward VII—and dealt with the problems when at the last moment the celebrations had to be postponed because the King was ill. In 1912 Eton Wick purchased a hose and reel for the use of the Eton Voluntary Fire Brigade and the following year erected a small mortuary in the village for use on the occasion of drownings in the Thames. Langley Marish provided oil street lights in 1902 and converted these to gas in 1906.

142 *Street   lamp lighting.*

Step by step the services and facilities which many people today take for granted were being provided—though the different parishes and districts were rarely in step. Bradfield Rural District started a refuse collection scheme at Bucklebury in 1902; it was the first rural authority to do so and a leading article in *The Times* paid tribute to the scheme. The refuse was tipped on suitable sites on Bucklebury Commons and covered by soil each day by 5 pm. It was the rural and urban districts which were responsible for building council houses after the First World War.

On a par with the rural districts were the urban districts and municipal boroughs, but above all of these—except the borough of Reading—was the new Berkshire County Council. However, compared with today, its 86 members had few responsibilities. They did not take over all the duties of the Court of Quarter Sessions, only the administrative—fixing the county rate, providing and maintaining the roads and bridges, managing the asylum for pauper lunatics, checking the accuracy of weights and measures, and controlling the spread of contagious diseases among farm animals. Meetings were held on a Saturday afternoon in the cramped conditions of the Crown Court where the only space left for reporters was in the dock. Even when, after 1914, meetings began mid-morning, members could still fit in committee meetings on the same day.

The workload, however, was growing as a succession of new duties was imposed upon the council. In 1902 it became the local education authority and four years later set up a school medical service. In 1903 the county took on the task of issuing road fund licences—over 96,000 a year by 1945. A new county surveyor was appointed in 1904 who was responsible for an improved system for the maintenance of the county's main roads, and by 1911 nearly half the money raised by the county rate was spent on roads and bridges. In 1929 the Poor Law Unions were abolished and the county council became responsible for the care of the poor—the able-bodied, the sick, the elderly, and the unemployed. The old Union workhouses were renamed Public Assistance Institutions, providing more than a thousand beds for the elderly poor. In 1918 the public health committee put forward a scheme to provide maternity and child welfare to complement the district nurses and mid-wives

143 *Eton fire brigade, 1906.*

belonging to the Berkshire Nursing Association. A county librarian was appointed in 1924. The county shared responsibility for the county police force, and in 1947 the fire service became a county responsibility.

The post-war years have seen the development of a very different, faster growing and more industrial Berkshire, served by a council with a changing rôle and responsibilities. In 1946 it became a planning authority, part of a system of nation-wide development plans to control the spread of housing, leisure and shopping facilities. On the other hand the formation of the National Health Service took away hospitals from the county's administration, just one example of the growth of the national control of services. In 1974 the whole structure of local government was reorganised by an Act of Parliament which transferred almost a third of the county to Oxfordshire and the southern tip of Buckinghamshire to Berkshire. It also replaced the boroughs, urban and rural districts with six large districts. Reading lost its separate borough status and for the first time Berkshire became a single unified county local government authority—responsible for spending more than three quarters of the money raised from taxes (rates or community charge) and central government grants. A hundred years after it was formed, the council had a staff of 24,000 and a budget of £405 million. It had also become the most important of the agencies responsible for providing services for the people of the locality. But for how long? In March 1995 it was announced that under the latest Local Government Review Berkshire as an administrative county was to be abolished, the only one of the old counties to be so treated. Let us be determined that Berkshire itself will not be forgotten and that the county collections of records and the hundreds of county-wide organisations will retain the name Berkshire and continue to serve the people of Berkshire.

144 *Baby clinic.*

Index